AMERICA

THEN & NOW

*Great old photographs of America's life and times
— and how those same scenes look today.*

EDITED BY DAVID COHEN

TEXT BY SUSAN WELS

*This book was made possible by a generous grant from the Kmart Corporation
in celebration of its 30th anniversary.*

KMART • WALDENBOOKS • BUILDER'S SQUARE • PACE MEMBERSHIP WAREHOUSE • THE SPORTS AUTHORITY • OFFICE MAX • PAY LESS DRUG STORES

HarperCollins
SanFrancisco

"There's an early afternoon calm in our town…only a few buggies on Main Street—the horses dozing at the hitching posts; you all remember what it's like…this is the way we were in the provinces…at the beginning of the 20th century."

— *Thornton Wilder, Our Town*

Summerville, South Carolina, by The Detroit Publishing Company, 1906

"*Future events, whatever they may be, will not deprive the Americans of their climate or their inland seas, their great rivers…their exuberant soil…[or] that love of prosperity and spirit of enterprise, which seem to be the distinctive characteristics of their race…*"

— *Alexis de Tocqueville, Democracy in America*

Experimental farm near Cheyenne, Wyoming, by J. E. Stimson, 1913

BY DARIUS KINSEY
SEATTLE

"I heard the mighty tree, its death-chant chanting…
In the echo of teamsters' calls and the clinking chains,
and the music of choppers' axes,
The falling trunk and limbs, the muffled shriek, the groan…
Clearing the ground for broad humanity, the true America,
heir of the past so grand,
To build a grander future."

— *Walt Whitman, Leaves of Grass*

Locomotive with fir log, Skagit County, Washington, by Darius Kinsey, 1926

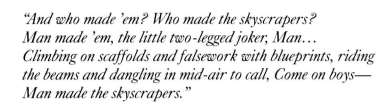

"And who made 'em? Who made the skyscrapers?
Man made 'em, the little two-legged joker, Man…
Climbing on scaffolds and falsework with blueprints, riding
the beams and dangling in mid-air to call, Come on boys—
Man made the skyscrapers."

— *Carl Sandburg, Good Morning, America*

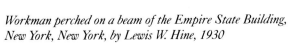

Workman perched on a beam of the Empire State Building,
New York, New York, by Lewis W. Hine, 1930

9

For information, please write to: HarperCollins, 1160 Battery Street, San Francisco
94111.

*The publisher and the editor have arranged to plant two trees for every tree needed in the
manufacture of this book's first printing.*

Library of Congress Cataloging-in-Publication Data

AMERICA: THEN & NOW/David Cohen, editor.—

     p. cm.
     ISBN: 0-06-250176-3
     1. American history—Pictorial works.
     2. Photography; artistic. I. Cohen, David 1955–

92-70492

92 93 94 95 7 6 5 4 3 2 1

*Tupperware™, Wonderlier™ and Pick-a-Deli™ are registered
trademarks of the Tupperware Division of Dart Industries.*

*The image of Mickey Mouse on the jacket is used with
permission of the Walt Disney Company.*

Two Hatchet of the Kiowa nation, photographed at the Indian Congress, Omaha, Nebraska, by Adolph Muhr for the Frank A. Rinehart Studio, 1898

"The Mirror with a Memory"

Even in these days of hand-held video cameras, when nearly everyone can make home movies in living color, the still photograph has a special power. It is the capacity to capture a moment in time and preserve it forever. In a world that is transforming itself at a furious and ever quickening pace, this is a precious power, indeed. Inside our own family album, there is a wonderful place where mother and dad just got married, the cutest babies never grew up, grandma is still young and lovely, grandpa, forever strong and virile.

When we set out to rediscover America with old pictures and new, we had no idea of the treasure that would be set before us. All over the country, there are carefully tended collections of these frozen moments—magic places where history comes alive before your eyes.

In an appropriately dark and hushed room in the bowels of The New York Public Library, a young scholar will show you stereoscopic images made by Eadweard Muybridge, the peripatetic English photographer who traveled America in the last half of the 19th century. Muybridge and his colleagues captured the ebullient life and unspoiled wilderness of a young country on glass negatives and paper prints. And there in the library, preserved in long, dark oak drawers, is their world of ghosts—a land where handsome men wear spats and bowlers, beautiful women in long dresses push wicker baby carriages, and boys in kneepants play stickball on the clean streets of New York. Don't get too attached—even the children are long gone now—yet their images live on, immutable and alluring.

Family outing, Boston, Massachusetts, by Charles H. Currier, c.1900

A collection of these spectral vignettes drawn from the last 150 years of America's life and times would make a marvelous book on its own. But we kept asking ourselves the same question: If we went back to the same places, tried to recapture the same scenes, what would they all look like now? And if these new scenes were juxtaposed with the old, what would we learn about the ebb and flow of American life?

As it turned out, there was a lot to learn. Did you know that prairie pioneers cut their sod houses from the hard dirt plain because there was no wood to be had on the vast, treeless frontier? And that each year, after the spring rains, their houses would bloom in a riot of wildflowers? Those who worry about the quality of modern Supreme Court appointees will be interested to know that Morrison Remick Waite, Chief Justice of the Supreme Court in 1876, had no judicial experience at all when President Ulysses S. Grant appointed him; he was a lawyer for the politically powerful railroads. The first automobile was not introduced to America by Henry Ford at the turn of the 20th century. There was actually a self-propelled vehicle, the Orukter Amphibolos, on these shores as early as 1804. Ford just saw the potential. He didn't invent the car. He reinvented it—revolutionizing the way that society produced goods of all sorts in the process.

That was probably the best lesson we learned: that the 19th-century French commentator Alexis de Tocqueville was right. The genius of America is in its ability to continually reinvent itself, to bring men, women and children from all nations and make Americans of them, to use their vast potential to light a beacon for the world. We haven't always been fair, nor have we always been right, but most of the time we Americans have been open to change. As you view the pictures in this book, we believe you will find that, much of the time, that change—progress, if you will—has been for the better.

W. L. Taylor of Cooperstown, New York, by Arthur Telfer, 1885

This project would not have been possible without the assistance and support of many people. Foremost among these are Joseph Antonini, chairman, and Michael Wellman, vice-president, of the Kmart Corporation, George Craig, chairman of HarperCollins Publishers, Clayton Carlson of HarperSanFrancisco, Barbara Loren, Sandy Kivowitz and a wonderful group of friends, advisors and well-wishers from around the country who are listed individually at the back of this volume. Special thanks are due to an exceptionally talented, hard-working and congenial staff. This book is dedicated to my wife, Devyani Kamdar, who always thought "Then & Now" was a good idea and urged me to undertake the project.

The real stars of this book are, of course, the subjects and photographers—then and now. In the old days, cameramen such as Mathew Brady and William Henry Jackson would roam the country using a marvelous new invention to show Americans their world—a contraption that Oliver Wendell Holmes called "the mirror with a memory." To make this book, a talented group of modern photographers—including Nick Kelsh of Philadelphia, Douglas Kirkland of Los Angeles, Ed Lowe of Seattle and Paul Chesley of Denver—took to the road in jeeps, vans and airplanes, retracing the steps of the itinerant photographers of old. If the old photographers set out to document the natural wonders and heroic achievements of a brash, young country, this new group set out to rediscover the country as it is now. We hope that by reading this book, you too will be able to rediscover America. Perhaps you can show your children and grandchildren what life was like in "the good old days," and you can introduce them to our ghostly friends from the old days—friends who never grow old.

— D.C.

When Congress decided to move the seat of government from Philadelphia to Washington, D.C. in 1790, critics called the proposed site "a howling, malarious wilderness." But the government moved anyway, and in 1793, construction began on the U.S. Capitol building, a Palladian structure designed by a young physician and gifted amateur architect named William Thornton.

Twenty years and four architects later, the Capitol was nearly complete. But then in 1814, both the Capitol and the White House were burned nearly to the ground by British troops who entered the buildings and set furniture, paintings, books and carpets ablaze. Reconstruction began the next year, and the Capitol wasn't finished until 1829, nearly four decades after President George Washington first laid the cornerstone.

"Big government" was an issue even in the early 19th century. Within 20 years of its completion, the Capitol building could no longer accommodate the burgeoning House and Senate staff, and construction began anew. This time the Capitol took its present, flamboyant, Greek Revival form, topped by a massive, 270-foot, cast-iron dome. Work was halted with the "wedding cake" dome half finished during the early years of the Civil War. During those years the building was used not only for legislative meetings, but also as a military barracks, bread bakery and hospital...

Right, U.S. Capitol during a halt in renovation, Washington, D.C., c.1860

I...n 1861, despite the pressing demands of the "War Between the States," President Lincoln ordered construction of the Capitol to continue as a symbol of his faith in the union. Two years later, when the building's nine-million-pound dome was completed, Thomas Crawford's statue, "Armed Freedom," was erected at its crown.

Renovation and repair at the Capitol never seem to end. Even today, a major reconstruction of the terrace courtyard is under way, with completion scheduled by Inauguration Day, 1993.

Right, U.S. Capitol, Washington, D.C., by Nick Kelsh

Union cavalry trooper, photographer and location unknown (carte de visite), c.1862

This Civil War trooper, with a six-shot Colt .44 revolver in his belt and an unsheathed light cavalry sabre at hand, may have been a member of the Union Army's 3rd Cavalry Regiment. The 3rd Cavalry fought Confederate troops as far west as New Mexico before moving to Tennessee, where it participated in nearly every major cavalry campaign for the rest of the war.

Even in 1862, the cavalry was largely ineffective against a dug-in infantry regiment. Rifles had developed to the point where infantrymen could pick off riders at 500 yards. This meant that the cavalry could no longer charge infantry positions, and their activity was confined to scouting and raiding, screening infantry troops behind them and fighting other cavalry regiments.

If the horse soldier, above, looks stiff, it is probably because he wore a metal neck clamp that kept his head perfectly still while he posed for this photograph—a three-minute exposure.

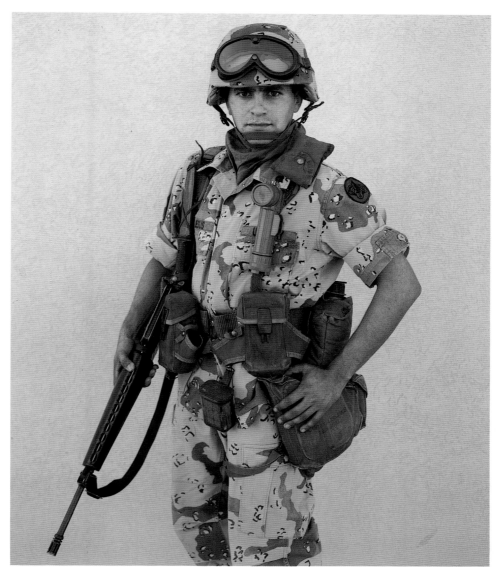

Specialist Cristóbal De Jesús Vázquez, U.S. 3rd Armored Cavalry trooper,
Fort Bliss, Texas, by Shelly Katz

The U.S. 3rd Cavalry was officially "unhorsed" in 1942, and today, the 3rd Armored Cavalry Regiment is a tank unit stationed at Fort Bliss in El Paso, Texas.

Above, Specialist Cristóbal De Jesús Vázquez, 26, wears desert camouflage, including a lightweight helmet, flashlight, first-aid kit and goggles. He carries an M16 automatic rifle that fires 30 rounds in 20 seconds.

When this picture was taken, Vazquez had recently returned from the Persian Gulf War where the 3rd Cavalry captured three airfields, fought Iraq's Republican Guards in two major battles and captured more than 2,000 prisoners, while suffering only one casualty.

*"France was a land, England was a people, but America...
was a willingness of the heart."*

— *F. Scott Fitzgerald, The Crack-up*

In 1866, Denver was the transportation and supply center for the booming Rocky Mountain mining region. Goods of all kinds were hauled in by canvas-covered Conestoga wagons along the crowded trails and stagecoach routes that ran through Denver.

The prairie schooners, right, identified as the "David Bruce Powers wagon train," had just arrived in Denver from Lawrence, Kansas, 560 miles away. The wagons circled in the 1500 block of Holladay Street (now Market Street) between F and G Streets (now 15th and 16th Streets). Horse-pulled wagons like these could average 20 miles per day with stops for watering and grazing, while slower, ox-drawn carts moved at a plodding 12-to-15-mile-a-day pace, depending on the condition of the roads.

Within ten years, the small, slow Conestoga wagons would be replaced by the mighty railroads, which held a near monopoly on long-haul freight transportation in the United States until after World War I. Today, most goods move in and out of Denver by truck. One of the trailers on the following pages can carry as much freight as three or four of the old Conestoga wagons; they can also make the trip from Lawrence, Kansas, to Denver in less than ten hours, while the wagon trains took nearly a month.

Above, Wagon train on what is now Market Street between 15th & 16th Streets, Denver, Colorado, 1866
Following pages, Northwest Transport Service, Commerce City, Colorado (near Denver), by Paul Chesley

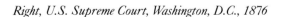
1876

"Scarcely any question arises in the United States that is not resolved, sooner or later, into a judicial question."

— *Alexis de Tocqueville, Democracy in America*

Although Article III of the United States Constitution provides for the establishment of a Supreme Court, it does not specify the number of judges. The high court began with only six jurists under John Jay in 1789, and during the Civil War years, there were as many as ten. In the 1930s, when the Supreme Court initially rejected most of President Franklin Roosevelt's economic recovery legislation, he petitioned Congress—unsuccessfully—to raise the number of justices to 15, so he could pack the bench with supporters.

In 1876, the court was led by Chief Justice Morrison Remick Waite (seated behind the draped table). Waite was a little-known railroad attorney from Ohio who had no prior judicial experience when President Ulysses S. Grant nominated him as Chief Justice. During Waite's tenure, the court, among other things, unanimously upheld state laws barring women and African-Americans from voting...

Right, U.S. Supreme Court, Washington, D.C., 1876

T
... he present high court is headed by Chief Justice William Hubbs Rehnquist (right, center), originally appointed as an associate justice by President Richard Nixon in 1971. The Supreme Court under Rehnquist, although conservative by modern standards, is no longer an all-white, all-male bastion. In 1967, Lyndon Johnson appointed African-American civil rights advocate Thurgood Marshall to the bench, and in 1981, President Ronald Reagan appointed female Arizona Appeals Court Judge Sandra Day O'Connor. When Marshall retired in October, 1991, after nearly a quarter century on the bench, President George Bush nominated black conservative Clarence Thomas to the bench. Thomas was confirmed, but only after the nation was riveted by a televised series of raucous Senate Judiciary Committee hearings where Thomas was accused of sexually harassing a female employee.

Right, U.S. Supreme Court, Washington, D.C. courtesy of the National Geographic Society

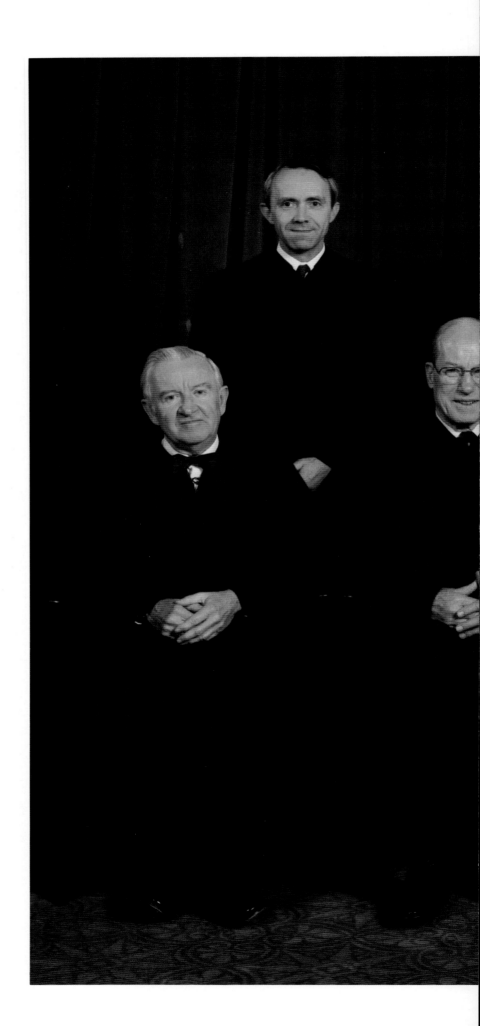

Saloon in Leadville, Colorado, by Virgil G. Jackson, c.1885

In the 1880s, Leadville, Colorado, was a prosperous, lusty mining town that knew how to have fun. Leadville boasted 23 restaurants, four banks and 97 saloons. In those days, rowdy customers would call for beer, whiskey and mixed drinks such as Buffalo Bill Cody's favorite, the Stone Fence (a shot of rye poured in a glass of cider, topped with a lemon twist).

By necessity, Leadville's pioneer bartenders had to shoot as well as pour. Their customers included Old Man Beebe, who "killed three bartenders and crippled two." (Old Man Beebe also killed the bartender who made that observation.) Less deadly customers included the Lundleys, who "always take what they want and smash things, but always pay," and a man named Jim, who "likes to jump on bartenders," but "never hurts."

Silver Dollar Saloon, Leadville, Colorado, by Paul Chesley

Today, Leadville's 113-year-old Silver Dollar Saloon still stands with its original bar, musk ox heads, spittoons and swinging doors. Owner Patricia Ann McMahon, center, bought the saloon 30 years ago and runs it with manager Carrol Nelson, second from left. Most of the customers these days are tourists and locals employed at the area's ski resorts. The most popular mixed drinks at the Silver Dollar include Hot Chocolate Schnapps, Margaritas and Irish Coffee.

*"Trees were so rare in that country…that we used to feel
anxious about them and visit them as if they were persons…*

*The houses were small and were usually tucked away in low
places; you did not see them until you came directly upon them.
Most of them were built of the sod itself, and were only the
unescapable ground in another form."*

— Willa Cather

With the lure of free land promised by the Homestead Act of 1862,
tens of thousands of East Coast settlers—as well as immigrants from
France, Germany and Scandinavia—streamed into the harsh, treeless
prairies of Nebraska. For most, the only material available for building
homes was the earth beneath them. Plows sliced up long strips of well-
soaked soil, which were then chopped into bricks and formed into
walls. Dull gray in the dry season, the cramped "soddies" bloomed
with prairie roses, weeds and morning glories when the rains came.

Philip Dowse, 84, still proudly tends the sod home his father built
in Broken Bow, Nebraska, in 1900. One of the early sod houses built
in Custer County, it is maintained as a museum and listed on the
National Register for Historic Places. Dowse spent nine years restor-
ing the house and still has the original plow his father used to cut his
home from the prairie.

Family in front of sod house, East Custer County, Nebraska, by Solomon Butcher, 1887

Philip and Eleanor Dowse in front of sod house, Comstock, Nebraska, by Paul Chesley

Above, One-room school, central Florida or possibly Florida Everglades, by Clark Ensminger, 1890s
Right, Students of the Marjory Stoneman Douglas Elementary School, Miami, Florida, by Nick Kelsh

In the 1890s, millions of American children in rural regions were educated in one-room schoolhouses like the one above, probably in or near south Florida's Everglades. Children of all sizes were taught by a single teacher, who was sometimes paid in pork, corn or whiskey. There were nearly 200,000 one-room schoolhouses at the turn of the century, accounting for 75 percent of all schools in America.

When school buses came into use, most states consolidated their small, rural schools into larger school districts—only 640 one-room schools remain in America today. In the 300,000-student Dade County, Florida, school district, students gather in the courtyard of the Marjory Stoneman Douglas Elementary School. Opened in September, 1991, the building has 42 classrooms for students from pre-kindergarten through fifth grade. The school was named for the 102-year-old "Everglades Evangelist" known for her tireless efforts to preserve the fragile environment and endangered species of the Everglades.

Legend has it that when Henry Hudson first landed in Manhattan on behalf of the Dutch East India Company in 1609, he was offered large quantities of strong drink by hospitable local residents.

The legend may or may not be true, but the fable captures the heady spirit that has characterized the city from its earliest days. Soon after Dutch governor Peter Minuit bought Manhattan island for trinkets worth 24 dollars (Yes, that legend is true.), the residents of Nieuw Amsterdam were already becoming known as great carousers. In fact, taverns accounted for over a quarter of the Dutch colony's total business, and the first city hall was established in a bar.

Even after the British seized the city and renamed it in honor of the Duke of York in 1664, its reputation for loose living and bad manners thrived. According to a shocked Anglican chaplain visiting in 1692, New Yorkers regularly cohabitated out of wedlock and loudly interrupted each other's conversations. The city's notoriety only increased when in 1702, British governor Edward Hyde, Lord Cornbury, was spotted cavorting about town dressed in a fashionable lady's gown. (Hyde also had his portrait painted in drag.)

After the revolutionary war, New York became the capital of both the United States and New York State, and George Washington was inaugurated as first president there in 1789. The national capital moved to Philadelphia in 1790, and the state capital went north to Albany in 1796, but within ten years, New York became the young nation's largest city with 60,000 residents.

Anticipating even further growth, city commissioners in 1811 devised a checkerboard layout for Manhattan, dividing the rural area north of City Hall into 155 cross-streets and 12 avenues. Although it may have seemed ludicrous at the time to divide outlying farmland into 2,000 unoccupied city blocks, the plan proved far-sighted. By the end of the 19th century, New York had absorbed literally millions of immigrants from Europe, and the city continued to expand northward as far as 180th Street...

...By the 1890s, Manhattan began to grow vertically as well. Several factors combined to radically change the New York skyline: The most important was the development of safe and speedy passenger elevators by Elisha Graves Otis and his sons. For the first time, office and apartment buildings could exceed six or seven stories. Also, Manhattan was a relatively small island with a comparatively large concentration of population and wealth—it made sense to build up as well as out. And, of course, there was the undeniable instinct to raise a building taller than the neighbor's.

In 1895, New York overtook Chicago as the home of the world's tallest skyscraper when the 21-story American Surety Building was erected. Four years later, the twin towers of the Park Row Building shot up to 29 stories. Then came the 60-story Woolworth Building, the tallest building in the world from 1914 until 1929. In 1930, the 77-story Chrysler Building took the title for one year, only to be surpassed by the 102-story Empire State Building—a name synonymous with "the world's tallest building" for over 30 years. The Empire State was, of course, inevitably topped—by the first tower of the 110-story World Trade Center. In 1974, the title of world's tallest building returned to Chicago, the original birthplace of skyscrapers. But by that time, New York's skyline—unparalleled by any in the world—had risen to intoxicating heights.

Inside this gatefold is a comparison of the New York skyline along the East River as it appeared 116 years ago and as it appears today. In both cases, the photographer climbed to the top of the Brooklyn Tower of the Brooklyn Bridge and made his picture in five sections. In the 1876 photograph, the bridge is still under construction—soon to become the engineering marvel of its age. Photographs are by J. H. Beal (then) and Nick Kelsh (now). In 1876, Mr. Beal sold eight-foot mounted panoramas printed from five 17" x 20" negatives for $25. The October, 1876 *Photographic Times*, said, "This picture will be highly valued for its historical interest in the representation of so many landmarks in the great metropolis in this Centennial year."—a prescient review.

Lighthouse with keeper and family, Pumpkin Island, Maine, by Charles H. Currier, c.1890

Pumpkin Island Light in Maine's Penobscot Bay featured state-of-the-art optical technology when it opened in 1854. Its Fresnel lens, ground in Paris, used prisms to focus the light of an oil lamp into a powerful, concentrated beam.

A one-legged Civil War veteran named Charles Leroy Babson tended the lighthouse with his wife, Georgianna, and two sons from 1870 until 1902. Although lighthouse keepers were given a small salary and a dwelling for their labors, their lives were usually hard and lonely. Often isolated on rocky, barren islands, they were exposed to severe weather without benefit of neighbors, schools or even soil for raising food. Some ferried dirt from the mainland just to be able to grow a few flowers or vegetables—knowing that a strong storm would blow their labors, and their sparse soil, into the sea.

Lighthouse with visitors, Pumpkin Island, Maine, by Jean-Pierre Laffont

Automated in 1933 as a cost-saving measure during the Depression, the Pumpkin Island Light was officially deactivated in 1934, when it was purchased for $552 by Senator George Harmon of Bar Harbor. In 1946, the station was sold to the Alexander Stewart family, who tended it as a private residence for 45 years. By the late 1980s, all but one of the once-manned lighthouses in America were completely automated and outfitted with radio and radar beacons. The figure of the brave and lonely lighthouse keeper slipped into history.

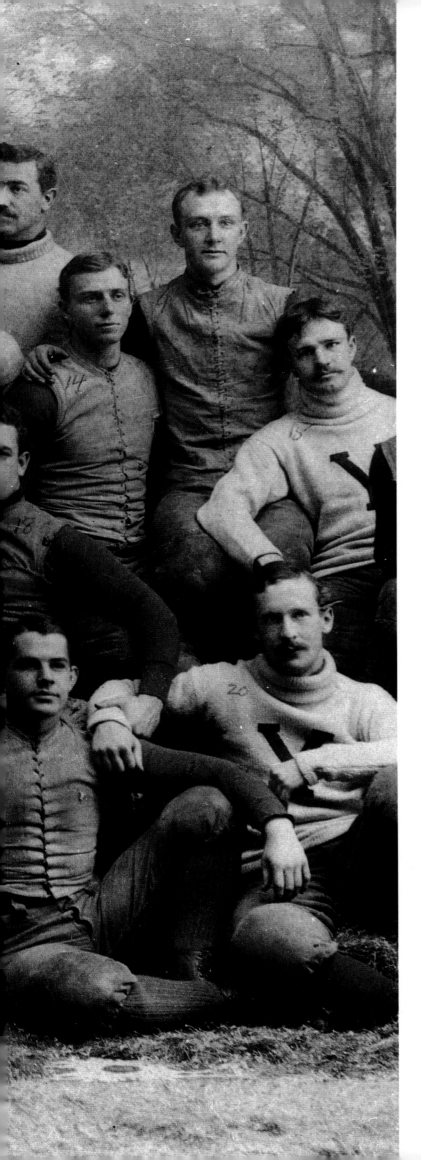

Left, The 1890 Yale Football Team, New Haven, Connecticut
Above, Nicole Gray, Captain, Yale Women's Fencing Team, New Haven,
Connecticut, by Sebastian Frinzi

In 1890, Yale's high-scoring football team, led by quarterback Frank Barbour (front row, far right) dominated rival squads, trouncing Wesleyan 76-0 and Rutgers, 70-0. The team lost only one close game that year, a bruising 6-12 match against Harvard.

The team's coach was football legend Walter Camp, a Yale graduate considered to be the father of modern football. Under Camp's influence from 1884 to 1914, the modern game was organized, and the first All-America team was selected.

In Camp's day, American football was more like a brutal cousin of British rugby than the sport that's played today. Players competed without pads or helmets in grueling, 45-minute halves with no rests allowed. In 1885, Harvard decided that the game was simply too dangerous and canceled its season. In 1905, 18 college football players were killed and 159 seriously injured, prompting President Teddy Roosevelt to call for some rule changes.

Today, Yale sports figures still pose by the same venerable Yale Fence. Women, first admitted to the university in 1969, took up intercollegiate fencing in 1974 and scored national championships in 1981-82, 1983-84 and 1984-85. Senior Nicole Gray, above, a first-team, All-Ivy pick, captained the 1991-92 squad.

Left, Bicycle messengers, Boston, Massachusetts, by Charles H. Currier, 1890s
Above, Bicycle messengers, San Francisco, California, by Chris Stewart

Bicycling became an American mania in the 1890s when enthusiasts traded in their dangerously unstable pennyfarthing bikes, left, for new "safety" bicycles with wheels of equal size. Despite warnings from the Women's Rescue League that cycling threatened young ladies' morals, women eagerly took up the sport. Some donned bloomers, while others kept their ankles from view by weighing down their skirt hems with lead.

Turn-of-the-century bicycles were used for business as well as pleasure. Messengers carried mail, telegrams and parcels to businesses and homes, often along rutted dirt roads that jolted and toppled the rider. In 1907, the United Parcel Service started as a foot-and bike-messenger business, and as late as 1940, most of Western Union's 20,000 uniformed messengers rode bikes.

Although their business was dented by the advent of trolley cars at the turn of the century and by the fax machine in the 1980s, bike messengers still career around San Francisco and most other major American cities making deliveries to law firms, ad agencies and banks. Today's couriers dodge traffic on 10-speeds and mountain bikes. Their "uniforms" run to T-shirts, headphones and spandex pants.

No. 3609. "VILLA OF BRULE."
The great hostile Indian Camp on River Br
near Pine Ridge, S. D.
Photo. and copyright by Grabill, 1891.
Deadwood, S. D

Left, Sioux camp near Pine Ridge, South Dakota, by John C. H. Grabill, 1891
Above, White Clay Creek near Pine Ridge, South Dakota, by Paul Chesley

On a cold, clear day in December 1890, the United States Seventh Cavalry opened fire on the Minnenconjou Sioux near the camp at left. As many as 200 Sioux lost their lives in the carnage.

The origin of the Wounded Knee massacre can be traced to the Ghost Dance cult, a spiritual movement the Sioux adapted from a Paiute visionary. The desperate, drought- and disease-ridden Sioux believed that the Ghost Dance could bring about a Messianic age when the living and dead would be reunited and the decimated buffalo herds would return.

Fearing the charismatic power of this new religion, General Nelson Miles of the U.S. Seventh Cavalry ordered the arrest of the Oglala Sioux leaders, including the great old chief Sitting Bull, who was killed in the ensuing melee. A few weeks after the botched arrest, the soldiers rounded up 350 Sioux, moved them to a camp at Wounded Knee Creek and attempted to disarm them. When a shot rang out, the cavalry opened fire, killing men, women and children at random. Ironically, none of the 25 original Sioux "ghost dancers" were killed, and they ended up touring Europe as part of Buffalo Bill Cody's Wild West Show.

Today, members of the Sioux nation still live on the Pine Ridge plains, above. In 1973, the American Indian Movement captured the village of Wounded Knee and held it for 72 days to call attention to their grievances.

The Tennessee River and Chattanooga from Lookout Mountain, Tennessee, by William Henry Jackson, c.1892

Viewed from the slopes of Lookout Mountain in 1892, the town of Chattanooga, Tennessee, nestles peacefully in the S-curves of the Tennessee River.

In the mid-19th century, however, a lot of blood was spilled over this site on Moccasin Bend. In 1838, Chattanooga was the starting point of the "Trail of Tears"—the brutal forced march of the Cherokee nation to Oklahoma under General Winfield Scott. Over a quarter of the 15,000 Cherokee died of disease and exposure during the journey.

Twenty-five years later, Chattanooga was the site of a series of crucial Civil War engagements, including the Confederate triumph at Chickamauga and the decisive Union victories at Missionary Ridge and "The Battle Above the Clouds" on Lookout Mountain. During that confused clash, Union General Ulysses S. Grant's troops struggled up the misty mountainside to victory against Confederate soldiers, who couldn't aim through the dense fog.

The Tennessee River and Chattanooga from Lookout Mountain, Tennessee, by Torin Boyd

Today, Chattanooga is still a busy transportation, industrial and commercial crossroads. Major changes in the landscape include the construction of what is now Interstate 24 (right, foreground) in the 1920s and the establishment of Moccasin Bend Mental Health Institute in 1961.

Above, Boating drill, U.S. Naval Academy, Annapolis, Maryland, by Alice Austen, September 25, 1894, 3:15 p.m.
Right, Boating drill, U.S. Naval Academy, Annapolis, Maryland, by Nick Kelsh

In 1894, above, midshipmen at the United States Naval Academy at Annapolis, Maryland, were drilled in boating on the Severn River. At the time, the school's 300 students learned both sailing and steam propulsion as part of their preparation for careers as naval officers.

Today, the academy's 4,300 male and female midshipmen still learn sailing and steam propulsion—as well as nuclear power, astronautics and international politics. The rowboats are gone, but midshipmen, right, train on the Severn River in 108-foot yard patrol craft.

The Davidheiser Force, Pottstown, Pennsylvania, by H. A. Abercromby, c.1898

In 1880, Pottstown, Pennsylvania, was afflicted by drunken roughs, rollicking party girls and rowdy mill workers who poured into town to work in the booming iron industry. Like many small American towns of its time, Pottstown had no police force.

An editorial in a January, 1880 issue of the Montgomery Ledger implored authorities to establish law and order, but it was three more years before $1,000 was budgeted for police protection. The constables who posed above in 1898 were known as "The Davidheiser Force," after Reuben Davidheiser, Chief Burgess of the borough.

Police officers, Pottstown, Pennsylvania, by Nick Kelsh

Since 1898, Pottstown has grown from 13,000 to 22,000 citizens, and its 42 police officers have a $2.6 million budget to handle the full range of modern urban ills from petty theft to drug violations and homicides. Pottstown is no longer a boom town, however. In the 1980s, the city lost major industrial employers such as Bethlehem Steel and Firestone. Now, Mrs. Smith's Pie Company is the largest employer in town (especially at pumpkin time), and small businesses fill the area's new industrial parks. Visitors to Pottstown can recall the heady turn-of-the-century days by strolling among the gas lamps, hitching posts and brick walks of the city's renovated downtown area.

Until the early 1900s, many farmers depended, literally, on "horsepower" to plow, cultivate, mow, rake and reap their crops. The Holt sidehill combined harvesters, at right, were pulled by as many as 40 horses and were designed for reaping the large, hilly acreage of West Coast farms.

Labor-saving devices like the sidehill allowed the average farmer to plant and harvest more than 250 acres of wheat per year in 1890, compared to only 15 acres in 1830. Still, horse-drawn machinery had its drawbacks. If one horse was stung by a bee and bolted, the rest of the animals could stampede and ruin the combine by stripping its gears. By the beginning of the 20th century, horse-pulled harvesters were largely replaced by self-propelled machines powered by internal combustion engines.

On the following spread is Dee Terry, a 74-year-old wheat farmer in Colville, Washington, north of Spokane. Terry can single-handedly harvest 50 acres a day in his $105,000 air-conditioned New Holland TR95 harvester. In fact, Terry and his sons, Dale and Dan, harvest more wheat in a year than Washington's pioneer farmers could gather in a lifetime.

Right, Holt sidehill combines in wheat field, eastern Washington, c.1900
Following pages, Dee Terry in New Holland TR95 Harvester,
Colville, Washington, by Ed Lowe

Philadelphia, Pennsylvania, Photo Illustrators Studio, c.1900

As viewed from the front entrance of Belmont mansion, the domes and spires of turn-of-the-century Philadelphia rose modestly above the green banks of the Schuylkill River.

Founded in 1681 by an ambitious English Quaker named William Penn, Philadelphia is linked historically with some of the nation's defining moments. The Declaration of Independence was drafted, signed and proclaimed in its State House (now Independence Hall). It was the seat of the Continental Congress during the Revolutionary War. The United States Constitution was drafted and signed there in 1787, and Philadelphia was the young republic's capital from 1790 to 1800.

A century later, when this picture was taken, Philadelphia was an industrial center and home to hundreds of thousands of recent immigrants from Italy and Ireland. Despite its burgeoning population, the city kept its skyline low for over a century with an unwritten agreement that no building would rise higher than the statue of William Penn atop City Hall.

Philadelphia, Pennsylvania, by Nick Kelsh

In 1987, after much dissent, the long-held general agreement to keep Philadelphia's skyline low was broken. The steel-blue, granite, 61-story One Liberty Place was the first to soar past the top of City Hall. The Bell Atlantic Tower, the Mellon Bank Center and others followed.

Across the river, Belmont mansion still stands in historic Fairmount Park. But much about Philadelphia has changed. Factory jobs vanished during the 1980s, and the three-century-old city is facing up to a whole range of modern urban problems. Still, many Philadelphians take the long view. Over the centuries, the city has weathered a host of catastrophes including British occupation during the Revolutionary War, the yellow fever epidemic of 1793 and the 1825 opening of the Erie Canal, which made New York America's preeminent Atlantic port. With their fine educational and cultural institutions, sports teams and business base, Philadelphians look confidently toward the future.

*"If I were asked…to what the singular prosperity and growing
strength of [the Americans] ought mainly to be attributed,
I should reply: To the superiority of their women."*

— *Alexis de Tocqueville, Democracy in America*

According to turn-of-the-century photographer Solomon Butcher,
Miss Sadie Austin, above, right, was not only an accomplished musi-
cian, but the best-known cowgirl in Cherry County, Nebraska. "When
her father was short of help," wrote Butcher, "Sadie put on a divided
skirt and rode the range."

Ranch women did everything, from cooking, cleaning and raising
children to pitching hay and driving cattle. Many carried six-shooters
and some shamelessly traded in their divided skirts for denim britch-
es which, wouldn't flap and scare the horses.

Today, in nearby Oshkosh, Nebraska, Jane McGinley, bottom, right,
splits her time between schoolteaching at Oshkosh Elementary and
helping her husband, Pete, herd and brand cattle on the 1,200-head
Blue Creek Ranch. McGinley is no drugstore cowgirl. She competed
in her first rodeo at the age of six and sometimes carries a shotgun to
kill prairie rattlesnakes.

Miss Sadie Austin, Cherry County, Nebraska, by Solomon Butcher, 1900

Jane McGinley, Oshkosh, Nebraska, by Paul Chesley

Left, The first World Series, Boston, Massachusetts, 1903
Above, The 1991 American League Championship Series, Minneapolis, Minnesota, by Joe Rossi

On October 13, 1903, the Boston Americans whipped the Pittsburgh Nationals 3-0 in the final game of the first World Series, held at Boston's Huntington Avenue Ball Field, left.

Boston, champions of the upstart, three-year-old American League, took the Series from the venerable National League winners in a 5-3 game upset. Since then, National League and American League winners have met in the World Series every year except 1904, when the New York Giants refused to play Boston.

Contrary to popular belief, baseball was probably not invented by Abner Doubleday in Cooperstown, New York, in 1839. Early forms of the game, evolved from cricket and rounders, were already popular by the 1820s.

A better candidate for the father of modern baseball would be New York City bank teller and volunteer fireman Alexander Cartwright. His team, the Knickerbocker Baseball Club, first played the game with flat clubs and a catgut-and-parchment ball in a Manhattan park, where they established the nine-player team and four-base diamond. Later, the game was limited to nine innings instead of lasting as long as it took for one team to reach 21 runs.

In 1991, above, the Minnesota Twins prevented baseball's first Canadian-American World Series by trouncing the Toronto Blue Jays in the American League play-offs. The Twins, playing in Hubert H. Humphrey Metrodome, went on to take the World Series from the Atlanta Braves in an exciting seven-game match. Minnesota's highest-paid player, center fielder Kirby Puckett, earned $3.2 million for the 1991 season (not including his $120,000 World Series bonus). This compares to an average salary of $3,000 a year for players on the 1903 champion Americans.

In 1904, the new operating room at the Johns Hopkins Hospital in Baltimore, Maryland, was opened with an all-star operation performed by Dr. William Halsted, the father of modern surgery. (His name is misspelled on the photograph.) Halsted was assisted by neurosurgery pioneer Harvey Cushing and three stellar proteges.

When it opened its doors in 1889, the Johns Hopkins Hospital radically changed physician training and medical care in America. At the time, most patients were treated in their homes, while hospitals served as asylums for the poor. Those who did seek treatment in a hospital frequently died from infection after surgery.

Operations were performed in open wards, and physicians' training was generally limited to a few months of formal lectures in undemanding commercial trade schools, which were not linked to hospitals. Physicians could begin a practice without ever having laid hands on a patient.

Founded by Baltimore merchant Johns Hopkins, the Hopkins Hospital and School of Medicine raised the standards for training and care to a level never before known in America. Students needed a baccalaureate degree for admission, and basic science requirements were rigorous. Bedside instruction was added to the curriculum, research as well as patient care was emphasized, and women students were accepted as equals.

William Halsted, considered to be a very slow and meticulous surgeon, was one of the school's founding physicians. He is widely known in medicine for developing the "radical mastectomy" as a surgical treatment for breast cancer. He also introduced the use of gloves during operations—though not to protect patients against germs, but rather to keep his nurses from developing rashes on their hands.

Halsted developed new operations for intestinal and stomach surgery, gallstone removal, hernia repair and thyroid gland disorders. Unfortunately, while experimenting with the anesthetic properties of cocaine, he became a lifelong addict and ended up in a hospital for drug-related mental disorders.

Halsted's assistant, Harvey Cushing, was the first American doctor to use X-rays in an operation, the first to correctly identify the role of the pituitary gland and the first to monitor blood pressure during surgery...

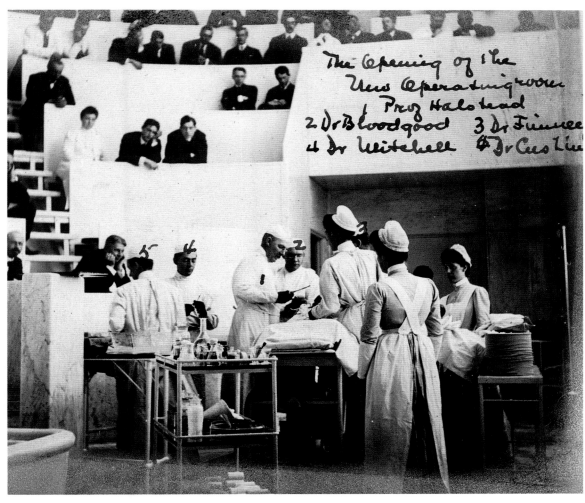

Opening of new surgical amphitheatre, Johns Hopkins University, Baltimore, Maryland, October 5, 1904

...Today, surgeons such as these at the University of Illinois Medical Center near Chicago have the benefit of countless new techniques that draw on miniaturization, computer, laser, ultrasonic and fiber-optic technologies. Using microsurgical tools, surgeons can reattach minute nerves and muscles of severed limbs. By harnessing sound waves, they can view internal organs and crumble kidney stones. Tiny cameras placed inside incisions can transmit images to television screens.

Right, University of Illinois Medical Center, by Mark Segal

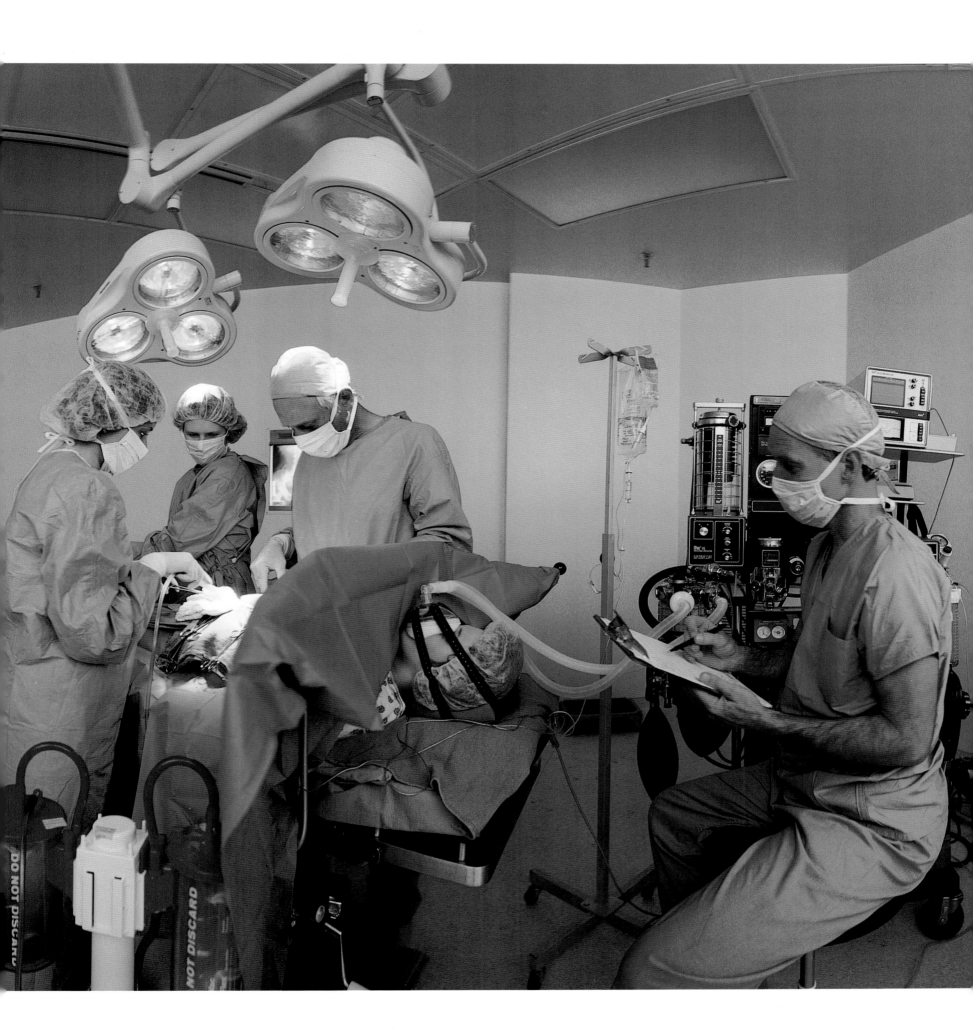

Left, "The Daring Ride of Mrs. Eunice Padfield," Pueblo, Colorado, by C. E. Holmbor (?), July 4, 1905

Above, Bungee jumpers, near Denver, Colorado, by Paul Chesley

Female daredevils were popular attractions in the early 1900s. Mrs. Eunice Padfield, left, performed a daring feat at the 1905 Colorado State Fair in Pueblo when she plummeted from a 35-foot platform on the back of her horse, Silver King. Mrs. Padfield earned $150 for the jump, and both she and the horse survived unscathed.

Today, outside of Denver, daredevils of both sexes get their thrills bungee-jumping from a bridge 100 feet above a Rocky Mountain gorge. Above, Christine Warren from Adrenaline Adventures of Denver dives from the bridge with 40-foot elasticized cords attached to her ankles. When asked why she leaps from high bridges, Warren told photographer Paul Chesley, "For the adrenaline rush."

Bungee-jumping, or something like it, was first performed in this country over half a century ago. A man who billed himself as The Great Peters or The Man with the Iron Neck tied an elasticized noose around his neck and swan-dived from a 75-foot rigging. He performed this feat successfully for over ten years until one fateful day in St. Louis when the cord snapped.

Above, Lumber barks and schooners in Puget Sound, Port Blakely, Washington, by Wilhelm Hester, Winter, 1905
Right, the Hanjin Pohang *docked in the Port of Seattle, Washington, by Ed Lowe*

When German immigrant Wilhelm Hester photographed these tall ships tied up at Port Blakely, Washington, in 1905, the mighty windjammers were already seeing their final days.

In remote Puget Sound, however, tall-masted lumber barks and schooners were still loading up with lumber and grain and setting sail for South America, Australia, Hawaii and Alaska. Hester made his early career in and around Port Blakely, taking and selling photographs of the great sailing vessels, their crews and especially their captains, who were the romantic heroes of their day.

It was an exciting and difficult profession. One January day in 1899, Hester photographed the crew of the bark *Andelana*, awaiting her cargo of wheat bound for England. Later that night, the ship capsized, and every man Hester photographed was lost.

Today, the Port of Seattle is still an export center for lumber and other forest products, as well as animal feed, aluminum, cotton and frozen vegetables—mostly bound for the Pacific rim nations.

At right, the South Korean ship *Hanjin Pohang* takes on her cargo of logs, lumber, cotton and hides, recyclable waste paper and scrap metal. Freighters like the *Hanjin Pohang* are twice as fast as the turn-of-the-century clippers, and one modern ship can carry more cargo than 12 of the old lumber barks.

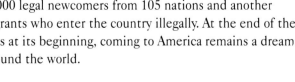

Left, Italian immigrants, New York, New York, by Lewis W. Hine, c.1905
Above, Undocumented aliens crossing the Mexican border into San Diego
County, California, by Susan Meiselas

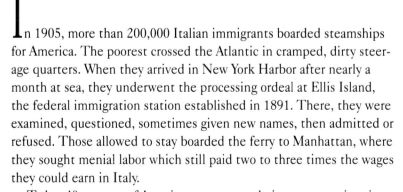

In 1905, more than 200,000 Italian immigrants boarded steamships for America. The poorest crossed the Atlantic in cramped, dirty steerage quarters. When they arrived in New York Harbor after nearly a month at sea, they underwent the processing ordeal at Ellis Island, the federal immigration station established in 1891. There, they were examined, questioned, sometimes given new names, then admitted or refused. Those allowed to stay boarded the ferry to Manhattan, where they sought menial labor which still paid two to three times the wages they could earn in Italy.

Today, 40 percent of Americans can trace their roots to an immigrant who set foot in this country at Ellis Island. Each year, they are joined by 400,000 legal newcomers from 105 nations and another 200,000 immigrants who enter the country illegally. At the end of the 20th century, as at its beginning, coming to America remains a dream for millions around the world.

73

Born on the "Golden Triangle," where the Allegheny and Monongahela rivers meet to form the mighty Ohio, Pittsburgh, Pennsylvania, was already an industrial giant by the turn of the century. At that time, the city produced nearly all of the world's oil, half of its iron and glass and two-thirds of America's crucible steel.

But this titanic productivity had a cost. Pittsburgh became a sprawling, smoke-belching, industrial city with smog so thick that street lamps sometimes had to be lit by early afternoon. When asked in the 1940s how he would improve Pittsburgh, architect Frank Lloyd Wright declared, "Abandon it."

In the early 1980s, thousands did abandon Pittsburgh—the domestic steel industry contracted and some 90,000 heavy manufacturing jobs vanished. But the city has, in many ways, recreated itself. Pollution and flood controls cleared the air and reined in the once-sulphurous rivers. Slums were razed, and parks and corporate plazas were built. Today, Pittsburgh is replacing steelworking jobs with positions in high-technology, health, research and education, and the city has been rated "Most Livable City in the United States" by *Places Rated Almanac*.

Right, Downtown Pittsburgh, Pennsylvania, from Mount Washington, c.1905
Following pages, Downtown Pittsburgh, Pennsylvania, by Nick Kelsh

"The clearest way into the Universe is through a forest wilderness."

— John Muir

The massive, old-growth trees of western Washington State lured ships and settlers throughout the last half of the 19th century. By 1905, the region's booming mills were cutting 3.5 billion board feet of lumber per year—more than any other state in the nation.

Loggers felled the huge trees with axes until the 1870s, when two-man felling saws appeared. Even with saws, however, it took logging crews like the one at right a full day to bring down a single tree and cut it into lengths that could be hauled to the mill by oxen, horse or locomotive…

Right, Hand-loggers, western Washington, by Darius Kinsey, 1906

... Today, Washington lumbermen Lee Hughes, Ray Kuper and Mike Winterringer can fell and cut a big tree in an hour with chain saws and powerful yarding machinery that lifts the timber onto trucks. Although many of Washington's magnificent old-growth trees have been cleared, replanting efforts begun in the 1940s are beginning to yield a second growth.

Right, Lumbermen, Orting, Washington, by Ed Lowe

The Dead Giant, Yosemite National Park, California, by Orlando K. Parker, April 8, 1907

In 1878, two woodsmen from Vermont named James and David Lumsden sawed and blasted a huge hole through the trunk of a 50-foot-tall California Giant Sequoia stump called the "Dead Giant." They thought it would make a great attraction for stagecoach tourists sightseeing in nearby Yosemite Valley.

For better or worse, plans to carve a refreshment stand on one side of the huge stump never materialized. But stagecoach passengers did get the thrill of careening down a hill through the 10-foot-wide gap, with just a foot of headroom and inches to spare on each side. When stagecoaches were replaced by automobile tours in the early 1900s, the drive-through stump remained a popular attraction.

The Dead Giant, Yosemite National Park, California, by Alice G. Patterson

Today, tourists Kevin, Susanne and Kendall Joyce and their friends can still drive through the Dead Giant on a one-way road leading from Crane Flat to Big Oak Flat in Yosemite National Park. The tree is one of only two tunnel trees remaining in the park, and the only one that the public can still drive through. The 230-foot-tall "California Tree," carved in 1895, is now off-limits to cars, and Yosemite's world-famous, 2,100-year-old Wawona Tunnel Tree, carved in 1881, was toppled by a heavy snowfall in 1969.

In the decades following the Civil War, many middle-class women turned their attention to self-improvement and community service. By the late 1880s, hundreds of women's civic, literary and athletic clubs had sprung up across the country.

The Owls, above, right, founded in 1894, comprised the first women's self-improvement group in Weston County, Wyoming. It was so named because its 16 members sought wisdom through the study and discussion of literature, art, music, history and religion.

Today, members of the Women's Civic League of Cheyenne, Wyoming, concern themselves with community service instead of academic studies. The 340-member club usually decorates a local home at Christmas time, and proceeds from the sale of crafts and decorations are used for community improvements. Last year, the organization raised thousands of dollars for groups including foster grandparents and battered wives, and they helped fund health care for low-income women.

The Owls Women's Club, Newcastle, Wyoming, by J.E. Stimson, September 6, 1907

The Women's Civic League, Cheyenne, Wyoming, by Paul Chesley

Above, Women's gym, Brown Bros., c.1908
Right, Gold's Gym, Hollywood, California, by Douglas Kirkland

In the second half of the 19th century, the ideal Victorian woman was pale, delicate and unlikely to engage in vulgar physical exertion. But in the early 1900s, some women were inspired to sweat and strain by fitness heroines like exhibition swimmer Annette Kellerman.

Dressed in tights and bloomers—or daring, form-fitting costumes like those above—they took to dumbbells, rings, rowing machines, Indian clubs, gymnastics, swimming and basketball. The public was shocked when some Vassar students played baseball. In a 1909 *New York World* article, actress Lillian Russell revealed that her daily fitness routine was to roll vigorously across the floor 250 times each morning—a technique that she claimed originated in a Turkish harem.

Today, at health clubs like Gold's Gym in Hollywood, right, exercisers Lynn White, Susan Arkin, D. D. Davis, Renee Richard and Illona Pagan (counterclockwise from left) trim fat and build muscles using a variety of modern contraptions including Stairmasters, treadmills and cable machines.

Track layer, Pennsylvania coal fields, by Lewis W. Hine, 1909

In 1909, Lewis Hine photographed this Polish track layer working
the grim coal fields of Pennsylvania. Many of the 13 million Poles,
Hungarians and other immigrants who arrived in America during this
period sought employment in the mines and mills. If they were lucky
enough to get the work, they hacked, blasted and shoveled coal from
dawn until dark, earning their pay by the 3,360-pound "miner's ton."
A full week of 12-hour days would earn them seven dollars.

Mushroom farmer, Kennett Square, Pennsylvania, by Nick Kelsh

When Guillermo Beauchamp, 61, immigrated from Puerto Rico in 1952, he fulfilled a long-held dream to follow his three sons to America. Beauchamp has picked mushrooms at Phillips' huge indoor mushroom farm in Kennett Square, Pennsylvania, since 1987. Twenty percent of the farm's workers are originally from Puerto Rico, and 75 percent are from Mexico. Workers on the farm earn up to $400 for a 50-hour week.

Above, "Little Fattie," St. Louis, Missouri, by Lewis W. Hine, May 9, 1910
Right, Joey Baldino, Philadelphia, Pennsylvania, by Nick Kelsh

Thanks to the wildly popular dime novels of Horatio Alger, the turn-of-the-century newsboy became a rags-to-riches symbol of hard work, initiative and thrift. In reality, the life of these young street vendors was not nearly so romantic. Many were homeless orphans living in the squalid alleys behind printing plants. Others were the children of destitute families who sold papers to help put food on the table.

"Little Fattie," above, was six years old and had already been selling papers for a year when Lewis W. Hine photographed him in St. Louis in 1910. Hine, now considered to be one of America's premier photojournalists, was a sociologist by trade. He photographed the plight of child laborers in order to support a campaign to improve child labor laws.

Today, most newsboys have been replaced by vending machines and adult sellers, but in many communities, home delivery still falls to industrious school-age boys and girls. Thirteen-year-old Joey Baldino, right, delivers the *Philadelphia Daily News* to 26 South Philadelphia homes every afternoon when he comes home from school. With tips, he earns about $25 a week, which he spends on state-of-the-art sneakers and other teenage luxuries.

Left, Breaker boys, South Pittston, Pennsylvania, by Lewis W. Hine, 1911
Above, Joseph Zieglar, Consolidated Coal, Enon Valley, Pennsylvania, by Nick Kelsh

In 1911, Lewis W. Hine documented the plight of the more than 1.5 million child laborers in the coal fields of eastern Pennsylvania. There, "breaker boys" as young as 10 or 12 worked from seven in the morning until after dark every day of the week, separating lumps of coal from slate. Bundled in ragged coats and scarves, they sat at the picking tables, covered in black grime, as tons of rock tumbled in a deafening, dusty roar down chutes into their little breaker room. While older boys could earn up to $3 a week, a week's wage for the youngest was only a dollar.

Many coal companies employed breaker boys until the 1920s, when labor laws changed and new sorting machines were developed. Nowadays, impurities are removed by equipment coordinated by sophisticated computer systems controlled by just one person, such as Joseph Zieglar at Consolidated Coal, above.

Left, First explosive aerial bomb, San Francisco, California, by U.S. Army Air Force photographer, January, 1911
Above, B-52 pilots and crew, Castle AFB, Merced, California, by Alice G. Patterson

In January, 1911, Lieutenant Myron Sidney Crissey of the Coast Artillery Corps, left, tested the first successful aerial bomb—a 36-pound explosive that he adapted from an artillery shell. Crissey dropped the contraption from a Wright Model B biplane piloted by Phillip Parmelee during a trial run near San Francisco.

The first use of aerial bombs in warfare was a primitive affair. Early World War I aircraft carried a passenger who simply pitched the bombs over the side. By 1915, however, German zeppelins carrying two tons of explosives were raining terror on Britain, and by the end of the war, 1,000-pound bombs were being dropped by multi-engine bombers.

Today, at Castle Air Force Base in Merced, California, above, Capt. Jim Bowles, center, Capt. Ken Ariolo, Capt. Mark Dibrelli, Capt. Glenn Carlson and Capt. Charlie Woodrow are pictured in front of a massive, eight-engine B-52G Stratofortress aircraft. First flown in 1954, B-52s still comprise the nation's primary manned strategic bomber force. With a range of over 10,000 miles and a ceiling of 50,000 feet, B-52Gs can carry 70,000 pounds of attack, air-launched cruise and anti-ship missiles.

Left, The starting line of the first Indianapolis 500, Speedway, Indiana, 1911
Above, The starting line of the Indianapolis 500, Speedway, Indiana,
by Ron McQueeney

The first major motor race at Indianapolis was a 300-mile contest held in 1909. The dirt and gravel track didn't hold up well, and two years later, the first Indianapolis 500, left, was inaugurated on a new track constructed of more than 3.2 million bricks. That year, Ray Harroun streaked to the finish line in his self-designed Marmon at an average speed of 74.6 miles per hour.

"The Brickyard," as Indianapolis Speedway came to be known, is now the world's oldest surviving auto racetrack, and although the original bricks were paved over with asphalt in 1961, they can still be seen at the starting line.

Over the years, the course has served as a laboratory for the American automobile industry. Innovations such as four-wheel brakes were first tested on its 2.5-mile, rectangular course. It is also the world's best attended annual sporting event, regularly drawing over 300,000 spectators. In 1991, Rick Mears won the "Indy" in a Marlboro Penske Chevy, clocking an average speed of more than 176 miles per hour.

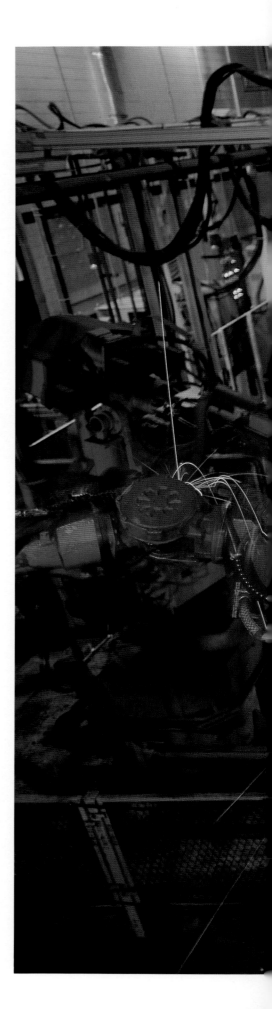

Above, Ford's first assembly line, Highland Park, Michigan, 1913
Right, Automated Ford assembly line, Wayne, Michigan, by Dana Fineman

Although the first horseless carriage—an amphibious, steam-driven dredging machine called the Orukter Amphibolos—appeared in America as early as 1804, the car craze really took off in the 1890s when the Duryea Buggyaut and Henry Ford's Quadricycle became newfangled toys for the wealthy.

Ford, however, knew he was onto something bigger than a plaything for the rich. In 1908, he introduced the Model T, a reliable, 20-horsepower contraption that rattled along at more than 25 miles per hour and was so simple it could be patched up with hairpins and chewing gum. By 1909, Ford had produced almost 18,000 "Tin Lizzies," at $850 apiece.

To meet soaring demand, Ford designed the first large-scale assembly line at his plant in Highland Park, Michigan, above, in 1913. Literally hundreds of manufacturers were producing cars at the time, but Ford's development of the assembly line and other mass-production techniques not only secured his company's future, but revolutionized the way society produced goods of all kinds.

By 1913, 1,000 Ford car bodies a day were dropping down chutes onto waiting chassis. The time needed to assemble a car fell from 13 man-hours to six, and the price of a Model T (available in "any color," Ford said, "so long as it's black") had decreased to $440 by 1914 and $290 by 1924.

Today, the assembly line at the Ford plant in Wayne, Michigan, right, is manned by 325 robots that perform brazing operations and nearly 100 percent of the body welds on Ford Escorts. Overhead monorails then carry the car bodies past human workers who install engines, electrical systems and trim.

*Left, John "Hubert" McDaniel, age 1, Lantry, South Dakota,
by Frank Cundill, 1915*

Above, John "Hubert" McDaniel, age 78, Arvada, Colorado by Paul Chesley

John "Hubert" McDaniel, left, was a year old when prairie
photographer Frank Cundill interrupted his bath.

McDaniel was born in a sod house in Lantry, South Dakota, built as
a homestead by his father and grandfather. Winters on the northern
plains were bleak, and at first, the McDaniels had few comforts or furnishings. Even their carpet was made from the tent the family lived in
before the house was built. Eventually, however, the small settlement
at Lantry grew, and as it did, the McDaniels started a general store
and post office in their sod house. Hubert's grandmother, Carrie,
became the town's first postmaster. Hubert, himself, worked 20 years
at a sawmill in the Black Hills of South Dakota before moving to
Colorado, where he maintained and repaired equipment at the
Keebler cookie and cracker plant in Denver.

Today, Hubert's grand-nephew David and his wife, Tammy, still
live on the old homestead only a few yards from where the original
"soddie" once stood. Hubert is retired and lives with his wife, Ruby,
in a house in Arvada, Colorado. Most mornings he plays cribbage at
the bar across the street and adds, "I usually lose."

1916

*"Under the moon, the back lot was thirty acres of fairyland—
not because the locations really looked like African jungles and
French chateaux and schooners at anchor and Broadway by
night, but because they looked like the torn picture books of
childhood…"*

— *F. Scott Fitzgerald, The Last Tycoon*

Inspired by a lecture given by photographer and motion studies pioneer Eadweard Muybridge, Thomas Edison patented the movie camera in 1887. The gadget didn't actually work at the time, and when it did, Edison decided not to project films on a big screen. He thought moving pictures had limited public appeal and instead developed the kinetoscope to show short films to one person at a time.

Within 20 years, however, millions of Americans were crowding small, storefront theaters called nickelodeons. There, 200 people at a time could watch a series of six or more silent, 10-minute comedies, adventures, melodramas and documentaries. Silent movie studios sprang up to produce films for these new theater chains and each, in turn, was sued—unsuccessfully—for patent infringement by Edison.

One of the first movie production companies was Vitagraph, which cranked out 300 short films in 1916. The filming of an anonymous Vitagraph production is shown above, right. The set is outdoors because motion picture film at the time was not very light-sensitive. Vitagraph would later become the first studio to use electric lights.

Vitagraph was known for its immensely popular but undistinguished comedies, murder mysteries, romances and action films. Movies such as "Captain Swift" and "The Broadway Bubble" featured movie sirens like Alice Joyce and leading men like Harry Morey. The studio was purchased in 1925 by Warner Brothers for $735,000. (It was probably worth about six times that price at the time.) Vitagraph's Hollywood lot later became the site of the ABC Television Center, home of the popular TV show *America's Funniest Home Videos*. Like the Vitagraph studios it eventually replaced, the show was successful because of new technology—small, relatively inexpensive video cameras that allow almost anyone to make his or her own short movies and send them in to *America's Funniest Home Videos* to compete for prizes.

Vitagraph stage set, Hollywood, California, 1916

America's Funniest Home Videos set, Hollywood, California, by Paul Chesley

Left, First self-service market, Memphis, Tennessee, 1917
Above, Warehouse club, South San Francisco, California, by Chris Stewart

Memphis entrepreneur Clarence Saunders revolutionized the grocery industry when he opened the first self-service market in 1916.

Until that time, shoppers presented their grocery lists to clerks, who picked and packed the items from shelves, bins or barrels. Saunders' new-fangled Memphis market saved labor costs for store owners and time for consumers. Although his fellow grocers predicted the idea would fail, customers loved it. By 1918, hundreds of Piggly Wiggly franchises had opened throughout the South and Midwest.

As to why the stores were called "Piggly Wiggly," one theory has it that Clarence Saunders was referring to the old nursery rhyme that begins, "This little piggy went to market." Saunders himself answered the question cryptically, "I named it that so people would ask me."

Today, the self-service market originated by Saunders has reached the peak of stripped-down efficiency in warehouse stores such as Pace Membership Warehouses and Price Club, above. Discount-driven shoppers pay $25 membership fees to enter the cavernous emporia stacked to their rafters with discounted appliances, car tires, electronics and giant tubs of mayonnaise. Prices average 40 percent to 60 percent below those of traditional supermarkets, and on a busy Saturday morning over 20 checkout lines process more than 300 bargain-hunters an hour.

Bethlehem Steel Company, Ordnance Department, Redington, Pennsylvania, c.1918

During World War I, the Bethlehem Steel Company opened a munitions plant in Redington, Pennsylvania, just east of the company's Bethlehem headquarters. A major supplier of cannons to the U.S. military since the 1890s, Bethlehem Steel retrained its Redington employees to manufacture artillery shells, aerial bombs and other up-to-date weapons of modern warfare. After the armistice in 1918, the plant stopped making weapons and converted to the production of marine motors, hoists, oil burners and valves.

Army Ammunition Plant, Scranton, Pennsylvania, by Nick Kelsh

Today, civilian workers at the Army Ammunition Plant in Scranton, Pennsylvania, produce 155mm artillery shells which are later fitted with explosives at the Louisiana Army Ammunition Plant in Shreveport, Louisiana. These projectiles, designed to travel 2 to 4 miles and destroy tanks or buildings upon impact, were used extensively in the United States' 1991 war with Iraq. The Scranton plant also produces state-of-the-art M864 rounds, which scatter multiple explosive devices over a wide area.

Union Pacific yard workers, Cheyenne, Wyoming, by J.E. Stimson, May 29, 1918

Soon after the United States entered World War I, 1.4 million women poured into the work force to replace the boys who went "over there." Women took jobs ranging from steeplejacking to mending railroad ties. These laborers at the Union Pacific Railroad's Cheyenne, Wyoming, freight yards did their gritty boilermaking, pipe-fitting and freight-handling jobs in coveralls, while their eastern counterparts labored in more "ladylike" aprons and ankle-length skirts. Although welcomed in the rail yards during wartime, the great majority of women either lost their jobs or were offered lower paying clerical positions when the war ended, and the men came home.

Union Pacific employees, Cheyenne, Wyoming, by Paul Chesley

Today, women make up a small but growing percentage of Union Pacific's train workers. These women at the company's Cheyenne freightyard are engineers, conductors, yard foremen, brakemen and switchmen. (Though the workforce has changed, the nomenclature has not.) They no longer have to shovel coal into boilers, but many of their tasks, such as coupling and uncoupling cars and driving spikes, are surprisingly similar to those performed by their counterparts in 1918.

Left, Sheep on South Lawn of the White House, Washington, D.C., c.1918
Above, Michael Lawn, White House lawn keeper, Washington, D.C., by David Valdez

When the United States entered World War I in April, 1917, citizens were mobilized in a mass conservation drive. Homemakers improvised wheatless and porkless meals, and crucial industries like railroads and power companies faced stiff government regulation of waste and productivity.

The Wilson White House also did its part. In a move to conserve gardening manpower, the President ordered sheep placed on the South Lawn of the White House to keep the grass neatly mowed. There was an additional public relations bonus: when the sheep were sheared, their wool was used to make mittens distributed to soldiers by the Red Cross. When the war ended in November, 1918, the sheep retired to less prestigious pastures.

Today, the South Lawn is kept green and trimmed by Michael Lawn, above, and three other National Park Service gardeners, who push Locke TriStar lawn mowers around the White House's 18-acre grounds. "It seems like I was born for this job," says the aptly named Mr. Lawn who has trimmed the presidential grass once a week since the last year of the Carter administration.

Left, Dance hall, Mengelwood, Tennessee, by Caufield & Schook, August 19, 1920
Above, Night club, Dyersburg, Tennessee, by Torin Boyd

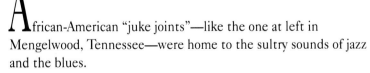

African-American "juke joints"—like the one at left in Mengelwood, Tennessee—were home to the sultry sounds of jazz and the blues.

In the early 1900s, African-American music and dances like the Cakewalk fascinated the American public at large, while appalling more genteel members of society. Fifteen female staff members of *Ladies' Home Journal* were fired for dancing the Turkey Trot on their lunch hour; a New Jersey woman was jailed 50 days for doing this "indecent" ragtime dance. To protect its population from "moral decadence," the town of Zion, Illinois, went so far as to completely ban the public playing of jazz in 1921.

No trace of the Mengelwood dance hall remains in the tiny Mississippi River community at Big Boy Junction, Tennessee. Today, the partying and dancing go on late into a Saturday night at Cleo's, above, a small but lively club in nearby Dyersburg.

*"Sensible and responsible women do not want to vote.
The relative positions to be assumed by man and woman in the
working out of our civilization were assigned long ago by
a higher intelligence than ours."*

— President Grover Cleveland

In 1848, proto-feminists gathered at the first Women's Rights Convention in Seneca Falls, New York, to hear Elizabeth Cady Stanton, mother of seven, read a "Declaration of Sentiments" asserting that "all men and women are created equal."

Originally associated with the temperance and anti-slavery movements, the campaign for women's suffrage made slow progress through the early 1900s. Before 1912, only six Western states— Wyoming, Colorado, Utah, Idaho, Washington and California—had granted women the right to vote.

During the next eight years, however, Alice Paul's National Women's Party, headquartered in Washington, D.C., above, right, mobilized a fourth generation of suffragettes into militant picket lines, parades and noisy demonstrations. The political tide finally began to turn. In 1920, nearly a century and a half after the founding of the Republic, the 19th Amendment was ratified, and the female half of America's population won the right to vote.

Today, the headquarters of the National Organization for Women, right, bottom, is a center for feminist activity in the nation's capital. Led by Patricia Ireland (holding the flag), NOW mobilizes a quarter million members in 750 local and state chapters around issues such as reproductive rights and the Equal Rights Amendment.

Headquarters of the National Women's Party, Washington, D.C., 1919 or 1920

Headquarters of the National Organization for Women, Washington, D.C., by Nick Kelsh

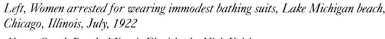

Left, Women arrested for wearing immodest bathing suits, Lake Michigan beach, Chicago, Illinois, July, 1922

Above, South Beach, Miami, Florida, by Nick Kelsh

In the 1920s, public beaches became a battleground of American morality. Modish women were dropping their coverups to reveal "skimpy" bathing suits, left, instead of the long taffeta swim dresses, bloomers and stockings that Victorian modesty had demanded.

Citizen groups decried the public beaches as "Sodoms by the sea," and lawmakers agreed. Signs went up at public parks and beaches detailing the legal limits of decent exposure, and white and flesh-colored bathing suits were banned. Policewomen, armed with measuring tapes, escorted violators to paddy wagons. But as the decade ended, the tide of public opinion turned. By 1930, new West Coast bathing suit concerns like Jantzen, Cole and Catalina were selling millions of form-fitting, knitted suits.

Since then, the bathing suit has grown and shrunk—mostly shrunk— according to the changing dictates of fashion and public morality. At South Beach in Miami, above, a policeman chats with vacationers Madison Straiton from Chicago and Julie Borovetz from Columbus, Ohio. Although their suits would have undoubtedly landed them in the hoosegow 70 years ago, these bikini-clad young women are not considered particularly risqué today. Although there is technically an ordinance on the books prohibiting topless bathers, they are, in fact, tolerated on Miami's public beaches.

Aerial view of Westwood, Los Angeles, California, Spence Airplane Photos, 1922

In 1922, San Francisco was the commercial and cultural capital of California, but Los Angeles was already becoming America's dream capital. Developers offered home buyers lots for less than $1,000 in the barley and lima bean fields west of glamorous Beverly Hills, and the new village of Westwood, above, was born.

Designed as a model community, the Westwood subdivision featured a whitewashed, Spanish-style commercial center. In 1925, the University of California chose Westwood as the new site for its Southern Branch— now UCLA—which opened in 1929 with 5,433 students.

Aerial view of Westwood, Los Angeles, California, by Douglas Kirkland

Today, the Moorish-style movie theaters and boutiques of the original Westwood Village are surrounded by towering high-rises, and the 419-acre campus of the University of California, Los Angeles, is home to 35,000 undergraduate and graduate students.

The California dream is changing, too. With over 9 million people, greater Los Angeles is now the second-largest—and the most ethnically diverse—city in America. Linked by freeways, the sprawling metropolis stretches from the ocean to the San Gabriel Mountains 100 miles to the east. Today, 1920s-era homes in Westwood sell for between $750,000 and $1.3 million.

Hollywoodland sign, Hollywood, California, 1923
Hollywood sign, Hollywood, California, by Douglas Kirkland

Originally, it was erected as a marketing gimmick to sell homes in the Hollywoodland subdivision of north Los Angeles. Later, in 1949, it was shortened to read just "Hollywood." But by the time the world-famous Hollywood sign was declared a historical cultural monument in 1973, it had suffered from years of neglect and disrepair and had to be completely replaced.

Playboy mogul Hugh Hefner hosted a star-studded fund-raising party to rebuild the sign, and a male rock star named Alice Cooper donated $28,000 to replace the last "O" (in memory, he said, of Groucho Marx). Construction of the new 45-foot-high, steel-and-sheet-metal sign was completed in November, 1978, once again marking the legendary capital of American movie-making.

Miami was a small, backwater town until the railroads arrived in the late 1890s, carrying carloads of northern tourists to a new luxury hotel built by Florida developer Henry Flagler (John D. Rockefeller's partner in Standard Oil).

But the sun really began to shine on Miami's fortunes in 1920, when developers turned 1,600 acres of mangrove swamp into a posh, new, Art Deco oceanside resort called Miami Beach. Almost overnight, Miami's population, prosperity and prices exploded.

From 1921 to 1925, the city's payroll soared from $140,000 to $3.6 million, population more than tripled and the assessed value of property jumped from less than $100 million to more than $400 million. So many northerners invested in the Florida land boom that a number of northeastern banks became concerned about a possible collapse.

In 1926, Miami's bonanza ended as abruptly as it began. Spiraling land prices led to rent profiteering, and the dock and railroad system broke down under the strain of excessive use. The capper was a deadly hurricane that killed 392 people and injured more than 6,000. Public opinion of Florida sank, and the Sunshine State entered the Great Depression three years before the rest of the country.

Florida made a comeback after World War II, with the development of air-conditioning, jet aircraft to bring tourists, frozen orange juice that could be shipped north and the dawn of America's space age.

Over the past three decades, several distinct waves of immigration have swept Miami. Northerners, many Jewish, first came to escape the cold New York winters in the '40s. Cubans fleeing the Communist revolution came in 1959. A second wave of 125,000 Cubans, dubbed "the Marielitos," hit the shore in 1980, and Haitians fleeing unrest in their country are still arriving. Miami proper is now nearly 30 percent black and over 60 percent Spanish-speaking.

Miami Beach—until recently considered a run-down, geriatric haven—is now a hot spot for trendy European tourists who cruise the hip cafes and clubs in its refurbished, pastel Art Deco District.

Above, Skyline, Miami, Florida, 1925
Following pages, Skyline, Miami, Florida, by Nick Kelsh

Left, Bootlegger's Model T seized near US/Mexican border, Marfa, Texas,
by W. D. Smithers, 1928
Above, Heroin seized in San Francisco, California, by Court Mast

The Temperance movement was a popular grass-roots struggle for almost a century before it became a victim of its own success. In 1919, bowing to pressure from groups such as the Women's Christian Temperance League and the National Prohibition Party, Congress passed the 18th Amendment to the Constitution and the Volstead Act banning the manufacture, sale and consumption of alcoholic beverages.

Almost immediately, the public thirst for spirits soared. New York's 15,000 legal pubs were replaced by 32,000 illegal speakeasies. Boozy "blind pigs," "beer flats" and "shock houses" flourished in even the driest Midwestern towns. The level of hypocrisy was dizzying: A 130-gallon-a-day whiskey still was discovered on the farm of the 18th Amendment's author, Senator Morris Sheppard. A jury trying a Prohibition case in San Francisco was found drunk on the evidence.

Organized crime moved in, and corruption flourished. Even honest agents had their hands full trying to stem the torrential flow of alcohol smuggled in from Canada, the Caribbean and Mexico in airplanes, ships and the secret compartments of souped-up motorcars.

Although the 21st Amendment to the Constitution repealed Prohibition in 1933, the same methods, and many more, are still used to carry smuggled heroin, cocaine, marijuana and other illegal drugs into the United States. Almost nothing surprises customs officers and DEA agents, who have found drugs in everything from ice cream cones to dirty diapers. Above, an agent guards 1,080 pounds of "China White" heroin—the largest seizure in U.S. history—found in a porcelain shipment.

Above, Immigrant family on Ellis Island, New York, by Charles Duprez, 1911
Right, Immigrant family returns to Ellis Island, New York, by Douglas Kirkland

Gazing southward from the Ellis Island U.S. Immigration Station, a boy shows his parents the Statue of Liberty in New York Harbor. This family was among 12 million mostly European immigrants who passed through Ellis Island into the United States from 1892 to 1954.

At right, Jack and Mia Freilich pose with their family on Ellis Island, which reopened in 1990 as the Ellis Island Immigration Museum. Jack, 81, a furrier, immigrated to America from Poland in 1938. Mia, 71, fled Hitler's Germany the same year. They met in 1946 at the Café Europe, a Manhattan coffeehouse, and were married three months later.

Ku Klux Klan parading on Pennsylvania Avenue, Washington, D.C., 1928

During the course of the last 200 years, the First Amendment guarantees of free speech and assembly have been regularly—and loudly—tested on the streets of Washington, D.C. In 1928, more than 40,000 members of the white supremacist Ku Klux Klan paraded on Pennsylvania Avenue to the Washington Monument in a display of anti-black, anti-Catholic, anti-Jewish and anti-union fervor. The scheduled cross burning at the base of the monument, however, was cancelled because of rain.

Gay rights march on Pennsylvania Avenue, Washington, D.C., 1987

In October, 1987, almost a quarter of a million gay activists marched down Pennsylvania Avenue to voice their demands for an end to sexual discrimination and increased funding for AIDS research and treatment. Participants unfurled a massive quilt on the ellipse across from the White House in memory of the 25,000 Americans who had already died of AIDS. By 1992, the number had risen to over 130,000.

Wedding portrait, New York, New York, by James Van Der Zee, c.1930

From 1916 through the end of the 1930s, photographer James Van Der Zee documented parades, weddings, street scenes and almost every aspect of life during the brilliant Harlem Renaissance—a period that saw a flowering of music, literature and theater in New York's black community.

The Harlem Renaissance gave rise to a literary movement that included writers James Weldon Johnson, Langston Hughes, Countee Cullen and Rudolph Fisher. Harlem theaters such as the Lafayette staged immensely popular musicals, including "Shuffle Along," which catapulted Josephine Baker to fame. Dramas like Garland Anderson's "Appearances" started in Harlem and then moved downtown to the Broadway stage.

Wedding portrait, New York, New York, by Douglas Kirkland

In February, 1992, Tracy Allen Clark became a bride at St. John the Divine Church on Harlem's 116th Street. An actress, Tracy says many of her friends in the visual and performing arts are moving back to Harlem from Greenwich Village because of lower rents and increasing cultural activity. Harlem Week, held every August since 1975, celebrates the neighborhood's music, theater and arts activities.

c.1930

Sculpted with pneumatic drills and dynamite, the Mount Rushmore National Memorial was created by the colorful and fiercely independent John Gutzon de la Mothe Borglum in the Black Hills of South Dakota.

Idaho-born Borglum studied art in Paris and was influenced by his friend, the celebrated French sculptor Auguste Rodin. Borglum's first attempt at a colossal sculpture—a depiction of Confederate heroes Jefferson Davis, Robert E. Lee and Stonewall Jackson at Stone Mountain, Georgia—was a bust. He worked nine years on the project, then quit after a financial dispute with his sponsors.

Two years later, in 1927, Borglum accepted a commission from the federal government to build Mount Rushmore (named after Borglum's biggest backer, a New York banker who gave him $5,000). He boldly predicted that the sculpture would take five years to complete. But the project took 14 years and was not concluded until shortly after Borglum's death in 1941.

The dimensions of the sculpture are truly monumental. Stretching 185 feet across, the faces of presidents George Washington, Thomas Jefferson, Abraham Lincoln and Theodore Roosevelt are each 60 feet high. (They represent, respectively, the founding, philosophy, unity and expansion of America.)

At first, Jefferson was to Washington's left, but the face had to be blasted away and put next to Teddy Roosevelt when a large fissure developed in the granite. Borglum also blasted a tunnel into the rock of a canyon behind Mount Rushmore which he hoped would house the U.S. Constitution, Declaration of Independence and other important documents. They were never actually moved from their home at the National Archives in Washington, D.C., but the solid rock hallway still exists.

Mount Rushmore under construction, near Rapid City, South Dakota, c.1930

Mount Rushmore, near Rapid City, South Dakota, by Paul Chesley

Above, Kitchen opened by Al Capone, Chicago, Illinois, 1931
Right, St. John's Hospice, Philadelphia, Pennsylvania, by Nick Kelsh

In Depression-wracked Chicago, where children were literally dying of starvation, it was mobster Al Capone and his gang who opened the city's first soup kitchens for the poor and unemployed. Less than a year after Capone's mobsters had savagely gunned down seven members of "Bugs" Moran's gang in the bloody St. Valentine's Day Massacre, they were serving up 2,000 to 3,000 free meals a day to the jobless on Chicago's South Side.

Capone, who had become immensely wealthy in the bootleg liquor business, was a populist gangster. In addition to the soup kitchens, he gave away 5,000 turkeys at Thanksgiving and threw a huge party for the poor in the city's Little Italy section at Christmas time. Not long after the picture above was taken, however, Capone was jailed for income tax evasion. When he was released eight years later, he was terminally ill with syphilis.

In Philadelphia, the dining room of St. John's Hospice, right, dishes up 600 free, hot meals a day to homeless men. Brother Stanley, St. John's administrator, says the hospice's clientele is younger than it was when he first came to the hospice in 1977. Today, many of the hungry men who line up for homemade soup, hot casseroles, fruit and pastry are in their 20s.

Above, Empire State Building with dome, New York, New York, c.1931
Right, Empire State Building with needle, New York, New York, by Douglas Kirkland

When it was first thrust skyward in 1931, New York's 1,250-foot Empire State Building surpassed the Chrysler Building as the world's tallest skyscraper, a distinction it would hold for over 30 years.

Unfortunately, the builders of the Empire State Building were victims of bad timing. They broke ground on the site of the old Waldorf Astoria Hotel just three weeks before the great stock market crash of 1929. The building was rushed to completion in less than 18 months and came in under budget. But by the time of the grand opening, the Great Depression was on, and most of the Empire State Building's 102 floors remained unrented. Fortunately, the skyscraper became world famous almost immediately, and the owners used admission fees from sightseers to help pay their taxes.

Over the years, America's archetypal skyscraper has worn two different caps. The first, above, was a domed mooring mast for dirigibles, a form of transportation that the builders predicted would be the future of transatlantic air transport. The fiery explosion of the German airship *Hindenburg* six years later dispelled that notion. In 1950, a 222-foot television tower was added. This proved a better bet and gave the building its distinctive, spired look.

"It is inconceivable that we should allow so great a possibility for service to be drowned in advertising chatter."

— Herbert Hoover, Secretary of Commerce, and later President of the United States, commenting on the advent of radio commercials

When radio took to the air in 1920, it marked the first time in history that someone could "broadcast" or simultaneously talk to thousands or even millions of people not gathered together in the same spot. The ramifications—political, economic and cultural—were enormous.

From the beginning, radio was hugely popular. At the height of the craze, one in every three dollars that Americans spent on home furnishings went for radios. From remote Texas farmhouses to Newport mansions, the country tuned in to voices and music that travelled through the air like magic. Even during the darkest years of the Depression, Americans kept buying and listening to radios. Jack Benny, Burns and Allen, "The Shadow," "Amos 'N Andy," "Fibber McGee and Molly"—all captured the imagination of listeners and helped them forget their troubles.

The news was more dramatic on the radio, too. For the first time, on-air correspondents could report news on the spot, as it happened. In the 1930s, live coverage involved strapping 30 pounds of remote relay equipment to the backs of a reporter, an engineer and a third volunteer. The three-man team, above, right, was from WPTF in Raleigh, North Carolina. Owned by the Durham Insurance Company, WPTF stood for "We Protect the Family."

Today, weatherman David Munsey of KTSP-TV, Channel 10, in Phoenix makes his live on-the-scene reports with the help of cameraman Dale Wright and remote engineer Mike Tomas. Their $120,000 truck beams Munsey's report back to the studio and then out to an estimated quarter million viewers each evening.

Early VHF radio remote unit, Raleigh, North Carolina, 1932

Television remote unit, Phoenix, Arizona, by Douglas Kirkland

Boone-Holden
Austin, Tex.

Left, Tom Mix and Frank H. Hamer, Austin, Texas, The Boone-Holden Photo Co., 1934
Above, Texas Ranger Maurice C. Cook, Austin, Texas, by Shelly Katz

In 1934, these two legendary lawmen, left, posed on the steps of the Texas State Capitol in Austin. In a picture entitled "The Reel Thing and The Real Thing," the photographer captured "Straight Shooter" Tom Mix and Texas Ranger Frank H. Hamer. Mix ("The Reel Thing") made more than 400 films corralling cinematic bad guys with the help of Tony the Wonder Horse. Hamer ("The Real Thing") killed 53 real men in the line of duty, participated in nearly 100 gunfights, was wounded 17 times and was left for dead four times.

Only weeks after this photograph was taken, Hamer (who was by then with the Texas Highway Patrol) cracked his biggest case: He tracked down and killed the notorious bank robbers Bonnie Parker, 23, and Clyde Barrow, 25. FBI Director J. Edgar Hoover called Hamer "one of the greatest law officers in American history."

Today, Captain-Assistant Commander Maurice C. Cook, above, and 95 other Texas Rangers travel around the state handling special investigations and high-profile crimes such as murder and armed robbery. "If the locals call us," says Cook, "we will assist."

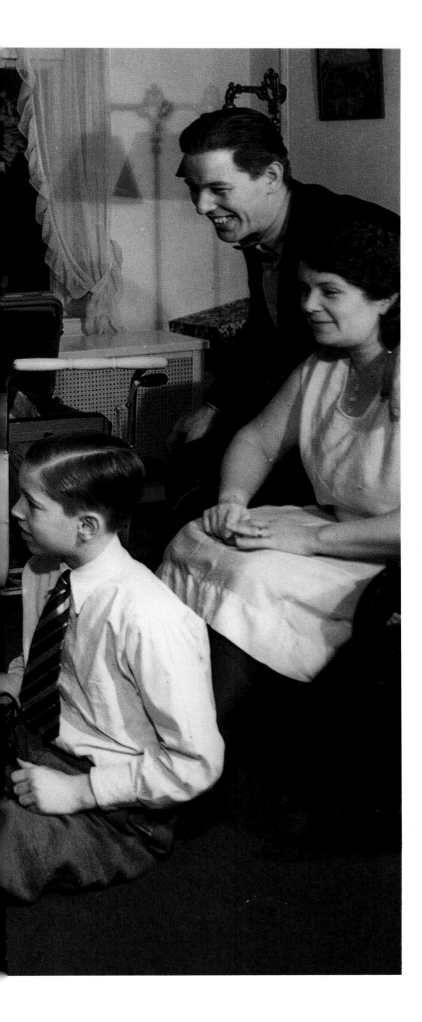

Left, Christmas morning, photographer and location unknown, 1930s
Above, The Weiss family, Grosse Pointe Shores, Michigan, by Dana Fineman

In this idealized view of a Christmas morning in the 1930s, left, wide-eyed children sprinted to the tree to find a king's ransom of toys. Little girls unwrapped Shirley Temple dolls and carriages, paper dolls, miniature weaving looms and cooking sets. Boys found "suedine" Lone Ranger vests, Buck Rogers Solar Scout badges, pocket watches, soldering irons, and real telegraph sets. There were lots of books for everyone.

As the Depression lingered on and unemployment continued at near 20 percent through the end of the decade, this picture represented a kind of dream for many families—something that could be done for the kids when times got better.

The Christmas scene, above, includes the stuff that a modern American kid's dreams are made of—an electric guitar and Detroit Pistons sweatsuit for Ryan, 11, Leggos and a "Grabbin' Grasshoppers" game for Allison, four, and a rocking horse and plastic motorbike for "Baby Doug," two. Of course, no Christmas in the early 1990s would be complete without Nintendo video games, Teenage Mutant Ninja Turtle paraphernalia, a Bart Simpson doll and those perennial favorites—Mickey Mouse and Barbie.

"When you build a bridge, you build something for all time."

— *Joseph Strauss, Builder of the Golden Gate bridge*

When it was completed in 1937, San Francisco's Golden Gate Bridge was the longest suspension span in the world. Its mammoth, 65-story center towers support a roadway 4,200 feet long above a treacherous strait linking the Pacific Ocean and San Francisco Bay. The Golden Gate's 36½-inch-diameter cables are still the largest bridge cables ever made, containing enough wire to circle the earth more than three times at the equator.

Workers under the direction of the brilliant engineer Joseph Strauss braved earthquakes, ice and precarious wind conditions to build the bridge. During construction, nine workers were saved by a huge safety net, earning them membership in the "Halfway to Hell Club." Ten others were not so lucky; they fell through the net into the icy waters below.

Those who admire the graceful sweep of the bridge have not only Strauss to thank, but the advisors to the Golden Gate Bridge and Highway District as well. In 1929, they turned down Strauss's original plans to build a boxy, steel cantilever bridge across the Golden Gate, and instead came up with their own design for what is, arguably, the world's most beautiful bridge.

Today, hundreds of tourists on foot and more than 120,000 vehicles cross the Golden Gate Bridge each day. Modern commuters coping with bridge traffic will be distressed to know that an average of only 25 vehicles a day crossed the Golden Gate during its first year of operation.

No bridge on earth is more exposed to the elements—from salt, rain and fog to winds that occasionally reach 60 miles per hour. To protect its 10 million square feet of steel, the bridge is always being painted. By the time painters finish one coat of the Golden Gate's trademark international orange (which takes four years), it's time to begin again at the other end.

Golden Gate Bridge under construction, San Francisco, California, by Charles Hiller, October, 1936

Golden Gate Bridge, San Francisco, California, by Alice G. Patterson

1938

"*Wanted: Young, skinny, wiry fellows not over 18. Must be expert riders willing to risk death. Orphans preferred.*"

— *William H. Russell, Founder of the Pony Express*

B y the 1930s, government postal delivery in the western states was taken for granted. No so, for the region's early settlers. Initially, the mail was a private—and precarious—enterprise. In 1860, the fabled Pony Express opened for business. Its riders braved deprivation, harsh weather and Indian attacks to carry mail across a 2,000-mile wilderness that included Missouri, Kansas, Nebraska, Colorado, Wyoming, Utah, Nevada and California.

Leaping onto fresh horses at relay stations with their leather "mochilas"or saddlebags, the heroic Pony Express riders cut overland delivery time by more than half, making the hard trip from St. Joseph, Missouri to Sacramento in just 10 and a half days.

Though it lives on in American lore and legend, the Pony Express lasted less than two years, giving way to the faster more efficient "iron horse." By 1864, the Railroad Post Office had begun operations, and by 1930, more than 10,000 trains were efficiently carrying mail to every small town in the country.

On June 17, 1938, Denver mail carriers, above, right, set out to deliver government bonuses to World War I veterans throughout the city.

The letter carriers, below right, in a Hollywood, California, branch perform many of the same sorting tasks as postal workers in the '30s. But main regional facilities are now using automated scanning and sorting technology to try to reduce labor costs. A first-class stamp cost 29 cents in 1992, a nearly 1,000-percent increase since 1938 but still just over half the cost of mailing a letter in France, Germany or England.

Letter carriers leaving on their routes to deliver bonus bonds, Denver, Colorado, June 17, 1938

Letter carriers from the Hollywood branch office in Los Angeles, California, by Douglas Kirkland

Daytona Beach, Florida, Le Sene Studio, c.1938

Daytona Beach in central Florida has been a popular spot for driving and dipping since the early 1900s when turn-of-the-century tourists took their carriages for salt-air spins along 25 miles of white, hard-packed beach. By the 1920s, wealthy car enthusiasts were holding races on the sand, and in the '30s, Daytona Beach hosted a 200-mile stock car race on a course that included a 2.5-mile stretch of seashore. In 1959, the first Daytona 500 was held on a new, asphalt track constructed near the beach.

Daytona Beach, Florida, by Torin Boyd

Today, cars can still cruise a ten-mile stretch of Daytona Beach. Traffic flows along at ten miles per hour in both directions—even slower during Spring Break, when thousands of vacationing students from all over the country crowd the waterfront.

Above, Shopping, Grundy Center, Iowa, by Arthur Rothstein, 1938
Right, Shopping, Southfield, Michigan, by Dana Fineman

The Depression-era prices posted in this grocer's window in Grundy Center, Iowa, above, may seem like unbelievable bargains today. But these were the 1930s, when nearly 20 percent of Americans were unemployed, schoolteachers earned $23 a week and steelworkers as little as $19 or $20 a week.

In those days, a dime could buy you a hot breakfast of eggs, potatoes and coffee. A new Pontiac coupe cost $585 and a modern six-room home with a two-car garage was just $2,800. A console radio was a splurge at almost $50, considering you could get a used 1929 Ford for just $7.50 more.

Today in Southfield, Michigan, prices for fruits and vegetables run between five and twenty times the old Depression prices. Freelance photographer Laurie Tennent, right, balks at the high prices of movies, clothing and travel, but considers fruit and vegetables a good buy. At the local Vic's Quality Fruit Market, bananas sell for 39 cents a pound—compared to seven cents during the Depression. Onions have gone up from two cents to 33 cents a pound, and sweet potatoes have risen from three cents to 49 cents a pound.

Chez Marie Beauty Parlor, Miami, Florida, by William Fishbaugh, 1939

In 1939, American women went to their local salons for hair treatments that included intricate pin curls and s-shaped "marcel waves," named for the 19th-century French hair stylist Marcel Grateau. Some gray-haired women even had their hair dyed blue. This became popular after a renowned Parisian stylist named Antoine tested the technique on his Russian wolfhound.

Permanent waves or "perms" were achieved by wrapping a customer's hair around dozens of curlers attached to electric cords in a sort of "Bride of Frankenstein" effect. The dryers at Chez Marie in Miami, above, were simply bonnets connected to a large furnace duct. While under the dryer, patrons of Chez Marie could enjoy a relaxing manicure. Dark red was the nail color of choice, with the tips and "moons" of nails left bare. A manicure or trim could be had for 50 cents. A marcel wave cost 75 cents, a facial, $1 and a shampoo tint, $2.50. Most women, at the time, would not think of having their hair dyed a different color, or at least would never admit it. And it is safe to say that any male customers who came into Chez Marie or any other women's beauty parlor in 1939 would have risked ridicule or worse.

Samy's, Miami, Florida, by Nick Kelsh

Today, fashionable Miami area men and women can come to Samy's for hair care, manicures and facials. Self-described "hairdresser to the stars," Samy has coiffed singers Gloria Estefan, Celia Cruz and Julio Iglesias as well as First Lady Barbara Bush. "But we treat every customer the same," he says, and that treatment includes free glasses of champagne and steaming Cuban coffee.

Straight, sleek hair is back in vogue, Samy reports, as are geometric cuts and warm-toned tints. The good news is that perms no longer require the use of large electrical appliances. The bad news is that perms at Samy's and other fashionable big city salons now cost $95 to $150. Haircuts range from $35 to $120. Hair coloring starts at $45, and manicures at $15.

Apache Bar/Casino, Las Vegas, Nevada, by Arthur Rothstein, March, 1940

Las Vegas was a dull desert farming and mining town until Nevada legalized gambling in 1931 and nearby Hoover Dam opened four years later. Off and on from that point forward, Las Vegas has been America's flashiest boom town—home to nine of the world's ten largest hotels and a mecca for the more than 20 million gamblers who lay down $4 billion at the gaming tables every year.

When the three-story Apache Casino opened for business in 1932, it was the pride of Glitter Gulch. The Apache featured Las Vegas' first elevator, and it was the place to see and be seen in the '30s and '40s, when the hotel drew big Hollywood names like Clark Gable and Roy Rogers.

Flamingo Hotel, Las Vegas, Nevada, by Alice G. Patterson

The Hotel Flamingo, above, was built 14 years after the Apache by mobster Benjamin "Bugsy" Siegel. Siegel was the only gangster who was allowed to have a casino license, because he was never convicted of a felony (though he had been indicted for murder). He named the Flamingo after his leggy girlfriend Virginia Hill. The hotel opened with a bang when headliner Jimmy Durante smashed a $1,600 piano on stage.

Norma Jean Andrew, Leonard Schutt and R. G. and Beverley Cooper, pictured outside the Flamingo, were visiting Las Vegas from Indianapolis and Surrey, British Columbia, respectively, when they posed for photographer Alice Patterson at 2:00 A.M.

"Heaven: The Coney Island of the Christian imagination."

— *Elbert Hubbard*

Brooklyn's Coney Island drew millions of sweltering, fun-seeking New Yorkers throughout the 1940s. With its hair-raising rides, sideshows and games of chance, Coney Island's amusement park and huge, white beach were New York's summer sandbox. On a hot July Sunday, as many as 1.5 million New Yorkers would crowd the waterfront.

Since the 19th century, Coney Island has alternated between periods of popularity and blight. First developed as a resort for the wealthy in the 1870s, it skidded into seedy disrepair by the early 1900s. Then, during the '20s, it was rehabilitated with a new board-walk and connected to Manhattan with subway lines.

By the early 1980s, however, Coney Island had once again sunk into decay. Although local treasure hunter Edward Armstrong, following pages, has the beach to himself on a hot October day, Coney Island's roller coaster fortunes may rise again as yet another generation rediscovers its parents' playground.

Right, A hot summer day at Coney Island, New York,
by Weegee (Arthur Fellig), c.1940
Following pages, A hot autumn day at Coney Island, New York,
by Jean-Pierre Laffont

Above, New England Thanksgiving, Connecticut, November 28, 1940
Right, New England Thanksgiving, Camden, Maine, by Jean-Pierre Laffont

Thanksgiving is America's most venerable national holiday. It was originally celebrated by the Plymouth colonists in 1621 to give thanks for their first harvest in the New World. George Washington proclaimed a national Thanksgiving holiday in 1789, and Abraham Lincoln made it an annual event in 1863.

In 1940, families like the New England clan above probably gave their thanks somberly. A black cloud of war hung over the world. France had fallen to the Nazis. The blitz was on in England, and President Roosevelt had just cut off all steel exports to Japan. It seemed just a matter of time before America would be dragged into the global conflagration.

The Thanksgiving meal, itself, may have included broiled oranges, roast turkey with celery stuffing, lima beans, and pumpkin pie washed down with Chase & Sanborne coffee. There was no televised football, of course. Both the National Football League and television broadcasting were in their infancy.

A modern Thanksgiving at the Rosenberg household in Camden, Maine, has many of the same elements as the New England Thanksgiving of five decades earlier. Family and friends are gathered together—roast turkey, stuffing, sweet potatoes and pumpkin pie are still holiday staples—and there's still a kids' table.

1940

"They go and they come with such regularity and precision, and their whistles can be heard so far, that the farmers set their clocks by them, and thus one well-conducted institution regulates a whole country."

— *Henry David Thoreau*

In the first decades of the 20th century, Chicago was the crossroads of the American rail system. Midwestern grain and meat rolled out to almost every corner of the country, and passengers on lines such as the Illinois Central, Topeka & Santa Fe, Rock Island, New York Central, Chicago & Northwestern and Alton all passed through Chicago.

Movie stars, celebrities and other well-heeled passengers could enjoy the comforts of a first-class hotel aboard luxury expresses like The Broadway Limited, which was staffed with maids and manicurists, or The Santa Fe Superchief, which treated guests to reading cars, afternoon tea and a nightcap before bed.

The golden age of American railroading began after the Civil War, opening up the American frontier for many and building great fortunes for a few. It was a relatively short-lived era. By World War I, the railroads' near monopoly over the movement of goods and services had practically ended. Private automobiles, buses, airplanes and trucks were all less regulated and better subsidized by the federal government. The railroads grew steadily weaker, and by the 1970s, ten midwestern and northeastern railroads had fallen into bankruptcy. The entire industry began a period of restructuring and consolidation. In 1971, 18 of the 22 largest passenger railroads joined the government-operated Amtrak system which now carries nearly all inter-city passengers.

Most of Chicago's passenger lines to the suburbs are now operated by the Metra system that fans out to Joliet, Aurora, Big Timber, Harbor, Zion and Fox Lake. Metra carries 70 million passengers a year on 1,200 track miles stretching east into Indiana and north to Wisconsin.

Outbound locomotives, Chicago, Illinois, 1940

Metra Line locomotives, Chicago, Illinois, by Dana Fineman

Kitchen, Ellsworth, Pennsylvania, Collection of Bethlehem Steel Company, 1943

In 1943, kitchen concerns were more about wartime efficiencies than decor. World War II was raging, the men were overseas, and at home, families coped with limited supplies of butter, shortening and meat. Growing vegetables in a "Victory Garden" was considered a patriotic duty—as was saving kitchen fats in tin cans. A *Good Housekeeping* article in 1943 reminded its wartime readers that the glycerine extracted from pan drippings could be used for TNT, nitroglycerine and machine gun bullets.

Kitchen, Pittsburgh, Pennsylvania, by Nick Kelsh

Today, working mothers like Dr. Pamela Weiss, a clinical psychologist in Pittsburgh, depend on a slew of kitchen gadgets that were unimagined in 1943. Dr. Weiss's remodeled kitchen includes a trash compactor, dishwasher, microwave oven, a cordless telephone and a self-defrosting refrigerator/freezer with an ice-maker that dispenses both ice and chilled water through its door. Daughter, Sophia, eight, shown here in her softball uniform, can help herself. Although fats and red meats are readily available, they have been largely banished from the Weiss's meals for nutritional reasons, and 50 years after World War II, families have started recycling again—these days for environmental purposes.

Rollout of 5,000th B-17 built by Boeing since start of WW II, Seattle, Washington, by Vernon T. Manion, 1944

World War II was won as much in American factories as on foreign battlefields. Above, hundreds of Boeing Aircraft employees celebrate the rollout of the 5,000th B-17 bomber they had built since the Japanese attack at Pearl Harbor only four years earlier. The B-17 "Flying Fortress" was a state-of-the-art, four-engine bomber with a range of 3,750 miles and a top speed of 318 miles per hour.

Boeing had come a long way since the company was founded in 1916 by lumber tycoon William E. Boeing. Then, it employed only 21 people, mostly carpenters and seamstresses who built and sewed the cloth skins of biplanes. By 1944, Boeing's 75,000 wartime employees were rolling out sixteen B-17s every day at a cost of $238,000 apiece.

Roll-out of Boeing 747-400, Everett, Washington, by Randy O'Brezer

Above, Boeing introduces the 747-400, the world's largest commercial jetliner. With six million parts and a wing area larger than two, five-bedroom homes, the giant aircraft has a top range of 8,440 miles and a cruising speed of more than 600 miles per hour. In 1991, Boeing's 141,000 employees produced five 747-400s a month, each selling for about $150 million, the cost of 630 B-17s.

Above, VJ-Day, Times Square, New York, by Alfred Eisenstadt, 1945

Right, Female prisoner-of-war returns from Gulf War, Andrews Air Force Base, Maryland, by Jean-Louis Atlan

When Japan surrendered in 1945, ending World War II, wild victory celebrations erupted around the world. In London, British and American troops formed a whooping conga line down Regent Street and into Piccadilly Circus. In Chungking, China, jubilant citizens jammed the streets, shouting *Mei-kuo ting hao*, or "Americans are swell."

In Times Square, New Yorkers exulted under showers of shredded cloth and paper tossed from windows by giddy garment workers. Photographer Alfred Eisenstadt covered the revelry for *LIFE* magazine. ("Eisie," now 93, still goes to work at the magazine nearly every day.)

The same rush of exultation and relief overcame America when the Persian Gulf War ended in March 1991. Soldiers arriving home at Andrews Air Force Base near Washington, D.C., were greeted with hugs, cheers, tears and waving flags, while a brass band belted out "God Bless America." One returning vet was Specialist 4 Melissa Rathbun-Nealy, the first American servicewoman to be taken prisoner of war since World War II.

Above, Diaper Derby, Palisades Park, New Jersey, by Cornell Capa, c.1946
Right, Gymboree class, Woodcliff Lake, New Jersey, by Nick Kelsh

Starting in 1942, the U.S. birth rate kept rising until it hit an all-time high of 4.7 million in 1957. Above, six of the 30 million "war babies"—the first wave of the Baby Boom—competed in a Diaper Derby sponsored by local merchants in suburban Palisades Park, New Jersey.

Today, the Baby Boom babies are 30 to 50 years old and have produced a boomlet of their own. Although a few Diaper Derbies have shown up again in malls across the country, infants and toddlers are more likely to get their workout at play and development groups like this popular Gymboree class in Woodcliff Lake, New Jersey. Gymboree provides exercise and games for babies and toddlers and gives young mothers and, increasingly, fathers, a chance to meet and exchange notes on teething and sleep deprivation.

Left, Jitterbugging, Porterville, California, by Bob Landry, 1947
Above, Dancers at the King King, Hollywood, California, by Douglas Kirkland

When the free-wheeling swing sounds of Benny Goodman, Artie Shaw, Glenn Miller and Tommy Dorsey swept the country in the 1930s and '40s, fans cut loose with wild, acrobatic dances such as the jitterbug, Suzie Q, Lindy Hop, shag and boogie-woogie.

From crowded Harlem nightclubs to small-town living rooms, young people like these couples in Porterville, California, swung, jumped and gyrated to jive tunes such as "Jeepers Creepers" and "Chattanooga Choo Choo."

Today, at retro hot spots like Hollywood's King King, above, neo-swing fans Mario DiDonato, Teri Stone, Michel Bergman, Laura Lacuira and Patrick Campi kick out to "gangster bop"—a '90s blend of swing, jazz, bebop and punk rock. "The music was great back in the '40s," says King King regular DiDonato, age 25, "and we've discovered it again."

Above, Roller rink, New York, New York, by Acme Photos, December 17, 1948
Right, The Roxy, New York, New York, by Douglas Kirkland

Roller skates were invented by an 18th-century Belgian mechanic named Joseph Merlin. Merlin's skates could not turn or stop easily, and interest in the sport diminished when the inventor crashed into a mirror at a masquerade party while roller skating and playing the violin.

By the 1860s, however, improved American-made skates had captured the public interest, and the first roller rink appeared in New York City. Roller skating hit peaks of popularity in the late 1800s and in the 1930s and '40s, above, when roller-dancing was in vogue.

Modern skaters can lace up their new rollerblades—and glide around the rink to hip-hop music at Manhattan's Roxy. Although most of the week it's a dance club, the Roxy is opened for gay skating on Tuesday nights and mixed skating on Wednesdays.

NOTICE:
THIS CLUB
IS NOT COVERED
BY LIABILITY
INSURANCE.

WARNING
SKATE AT YOUR
OWN RISK...
NOT RESPONSIBLE
FOR ACCIDENTS...

Roxy MGT.

Above, La Guardia Airport, New York, New York, by H. Armstrong Roberts II, c.1949
Right, La Guardia Airport, New York, New York, by Douglas Kirkland

La Guardia Airport opened to commercial traffic on December 2, 1939, just in time for the New York World's Fair. Named after Fiorello La Guardia, the popular New York mayor of that time, it was built on the site of the old Gala Amusement Park.

When La Guardia first opened, families drove over on Sunday afternoons just to watch the planes take off and land. Airport passengers were mostly wealthy adventurers travelling to Europe on transatlantic "clipper" aircraft—sea planes that could make ocean landings if necessary.

Over the years, as air travel became more accessible to the middle class, traffic boomed at La Guardia. By the time the picture above was taken, the airport was processing over three million passengers and nearly 160,000 takeoffs and landings each year.

Now, annual passenger traffic has increased nearly ten-fold, and there are few reminders left of the time when every airplane trip was a glamorous adventure.

1950

On July 24, 1950, photographers chronicled the ascent of Bumper 8, the first rocket to take off from the new American launch facility at Cape Canaveral, Florida. Although the United States has two other launch sites in California and Virginia, Cape Canaveral and its Kennedy Space Center have been the focal point of the American space effort for the past four decades.

The space race began in earnest on October 5, 1957, when the Soviets put Sputnik 1—a two-foot diameter sphere—into orbit. This was followed less than a month later by Sputnik 2—a 1,000-pound satellite carrying a live dog named Laika. A month later, the first U.S. attempt to put a puny six-inch satellite into orbit exploded on the launch pad.

In the context of the Cold War, these early Soviet successes—and the spectacular American failure—took on cosmic significance. The Soviet rockets could deliver satellites into orbit (and atomic weapons to America); ours blew up on the pad. U.S. politicians reacted by converting the National Advisory Committee for Aeronautics (NACA) into the National Aeronautics and Space Administration (NASA) in 1958. And from that point forward, Saturn rockets and "right stuff" astronauts became a national passion. On July 20, 1969, the United States "won" the space race by fulfilling President Kennedy's 1961 promise to put a man on the moon by the end of the decade.

Today, the American manned space program is more pragmatic than symbolic. Reusable space shuttles ferry satellites and payload specialists in and out of earth orbit, and space shots seem nearly commonplace. Only when the 25th shuttle flight erupted into a fireball on January 28, 1986, killing all aboard, was the country reminded that risk and heroism were still part of the mission.

First rocket launch from Cape Canaveral, Florida, General Electric and U.S. Army Ordnance, July 24, 1950

Space Shuttle launch, Cape Canaveral, Florida, by Roger Scruggs

Left, Elementary school, photographer and location unknown, 1950s
Above, Redwood Country Day School, Rohnert Park, California, by Jay O'Neil

In the late 1950s, America's Cold War jitters extended to the nation's classrooms. Compared with the Soviet Union, fretted *LIFE* magazine in 1958, U.S. schools suffered from inferior curriculums and overcrowded classrooms, producing students who were poorly prepared for the Space Age.

Today, schools are again being criticized for producing students who are unprepared for the global information age. A report from the Educational Testing Service found that 90 percent of American students had test scores below the averages of other industrial nations in science and math.

In Rohnert Park, California, north of San Francisco, parents pay over $3,000 per year to send their children to progressive Redwood Country Day School, above. There, children as young as five learn computer fundamentals. "The children here really seem to enjoy school much more than we did," says principal Susan Hicks.

Aerial view of Levittown, New York, c.1951

When World War II ended, hundreds of thousands of victorious young war veterans came home to new wives, new babies and no affordable housing. Developer William Levitt stepped in to meet this need with an audacious and typically American scheme. If cars, tanks and airplanes could be mass produced, why not houses?

From 1947 to 1951, Levitt and Sons turned 1,200 acres of Long Island potato fields into a brand new, planned community complete with schools, shopping centers, community centers and playgrounds. Over 17,000 prefabricated, four-room houses were built at the break-neck rate of 12 houses per day.

The $8,000 Levitt house included a TV, washing machine and out-door barbecue. Levittown homes were sold to white veterans only, and for as little as $20 down. The concept was so successful in New York that Levittown, Pennsylvania, outside Philadelphia, was begun the next year.

Aerial view of Levittown, New York, by Jean-Pierre Laffont

Over the past 45 years, the cookie-cutter Levitt houses have been remodeled into Swiss chalets, American colonials or Tudor manors. Trees, shrubs and lawns cover the old potato fields, and grandchildren of the young GIs who bought the original Levittown houses play in their yards. Remodeled or expanded homes now sell for $160,000 or more, and few of the original ranch and Cape Cod models, with their white metal kitchen cabinets and distinctive Levittown door knockers, remain. Ironically, these are now considered historic landmarks— the last of the original tract houses.

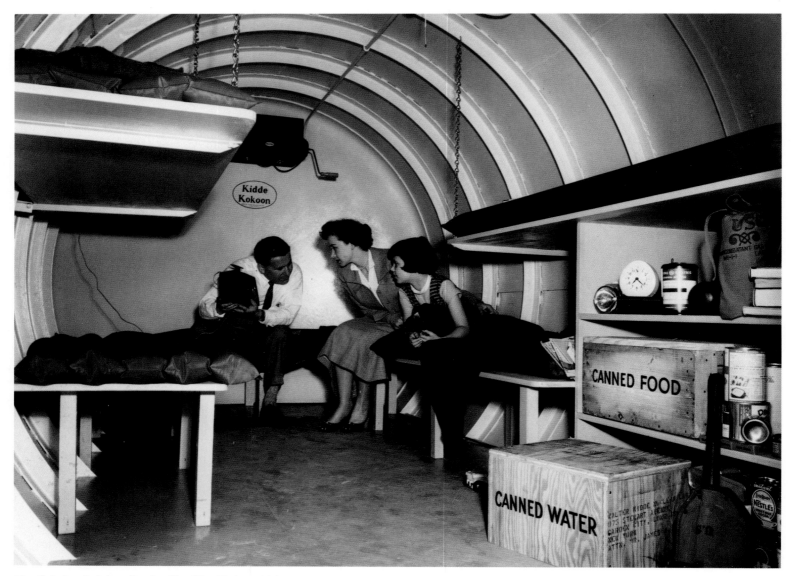

Family in bomb shelter, Garden City, New York, c.1955

After the widely publicized American hydrogen bomb tests at Bikini Atoll in 1954 and the establishment of the communist Warsaw Pact in 1955, the "Cold War" between the United States and the Soviet Union seemed to be heating up. Schools across America held "duck and cover" drills—apparently under the assumption that school desks could provide protection from Soviet hydrogen bombs—and some families began to build well-stocked basement bomb shelters.

This widespread fear of atomic attack and fallout created opportunities for marketers such as Walter Kidde Nuclear Laboratories of Garden City, Long Island. Their state-of-the-art Kidde Kokoon was guaranteed to keep a family safe three feet underground during a nuclear attack.

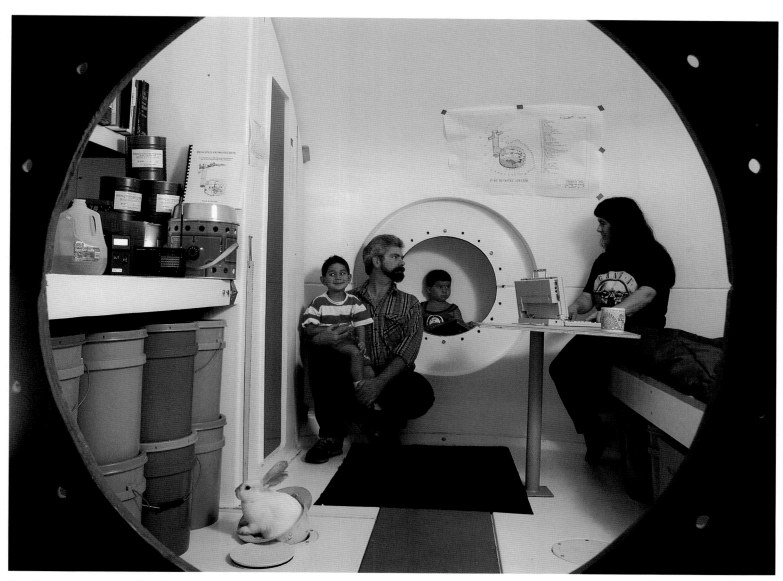

Family in disaster shelter, New Preston, Connecticut, by Jean-Pierre Laffont

Today, families that want protection from nuclear, biological and chemical attack, hurricanes and earthquakes can spend $22,000 for an ES-10 Disaster Shelter, developed by Subtech of Northwood, New Hampshire. Buried 15½ feet below the ground, the shelter comes equipped with a command station, decontamination area and optional nuclear, biological and chemical warfare filters. The ES-10 can protect 10 people for 30 days after a major disaster—man-made or natural—and comes with a 30-year warranty. Walton McCarthy, Subtech's president and chief engineer says, "Among our best customers are U.S. Senators and Congressmen, government economic analysts and the IRS, which has contingency plans to collect taxes after an atomic attack."

Left, Children watching "Davy Crockett," by Francis Miller, 1955

Above, Children with Teenage Mutant Ninja Turtles video game, Dallas, Texas, by Shelly Katz

In December 1945, 81 percent of Gallup Poll respondents said they had never seen TV. Six years later, ten million American families owned sets.

Americans demonstrated a huge appetite for shows such as "I Love Lucy," "The Lone Ranger" and "Kukla, Fran and Ollie." In 1950, children were watching an average of 27 hours of television a week—slightly more than they watch now. Boston University President Daniel Marsh lamented, "We are destined to have a nation of morons."

In 1955, left, young baby boomers were entertained by "Davy Crockett," "Gunsmoke" and "Captain Kangaroo." (That's Fess Parker as Davy Crockett on the screen.) The modern four-year-old Teenage Mutant Ninja Turtle fans, above, have far more options than their parents had. They can choose among four broadcast networks, two dozen cable channels, videotaped movies and interactive video games, as well as compact disks that project video encyclopedias and books onto their screens.

Left, Debbie Reynolds with Lincoln Futura, photographer and location unknown, c.1955.

Above, General Motors Ultralite, Warren, Michigan

In 1955, posh partygoers, left, ogled the Ford Lincoln Futura, touted as "the most revolutionary car to appear on the American road in the last decade." The futuristic model featured two totally sound-proofed and climate-controlled cockpits for driver and passenger, who could communicate with microphones. Although it was never actually seen on America's highways, the Futura did became familiar to a generation of '60s TV watchers as the Batmobile.

The Futura was one of dozens of dream cars concocted by imaginative automotive designers in Detroit. General Motors thrilled audiences in the 1950s with its "Motorama" extravaganzas, which featured outlandish cars of the future, driven by Mr. and Mrs. Tomorrow. Aerospace fantasy cars—with rocket-like taillights or fighter-plane-like nose cones—were especially popular and reached their apex with the 1956 Ford Volante Tri-Athodyne, an imaginary sportscar that would lift off the ground and fly.

Some futuristic '50s and '60s dream cars toyed with alternative fuel sources. Designs for the 1958 Ford Nucleon, for example, featured a rechargeable atomic reactor in the rear. In more recent years, however, concept cars have become decidedly more practical. The General Motors Ultralite, above, was unveiled at the 1992 Detroit North American International Auto Show. The sedan weighs in at just 1,400 pounds and is designed to get up to 100 miles to the gallon.

First there was the hamburger, then the car (or was it the other way around?). Anyway, when the two concepts collided in the 1940s, the drive-in diner was born. The result was irresistible to teenagers. Postwar, southern high-schoolers would "go frogging" (cruising) and scarf hamburgers after a ball game. In the '50s, "carhops"—sometimes on roller skates—would deliver fresh orders of burgers, fries, fried chicken and shakes right to the car door. A few eateries, like Ott's in San Francisco, had their own mini-transmitters so the kids could select songs on the jukebox inside and listen to them on their car radios in the parking lot.

Right, Drive-in diner, suburban Washington, D.C., by Hank Walker, 1956

Although there are still some great old diners around, they now trade mostly in nostalgia. The great mass of burger-gulping kids patronize mass-market chains like McDonald's. The first of what is now 12,150 McDonald's opened in 1955. McDonald's cut out frills like carhops and long menus, but with 15-cent burgers and 25-cent shakes, the concept caught on. Over 40 years later, teens from Seattle's Ingram and Nathan Hale High still drive over to the local McDonald's, which serves up to 1,500 burgers and 355 pounds of fries a day. You can still order from your car, of course, but nowadays it's through an intercom.

Right, Teenagers at McDonald's, Northgate Way, Seattle, Washington, by Ed Lowe

Left, Wedding, Louisville, Kentucky, by Lin Caufield, 1956
Above, Wedding, Atlanta, Georgia, by Nick Kelsh

In 1956, more than three million American couples tied the knot. Elaborate and traditional nuptials, like the Louisville, Kentucky, wedding of Dorothy Zapp, left, were the '50s fashion in contrast with the no-frills, impulse weddings of the wartime 1940s.

Brides and grooms were also younger—and some thought more unprepared—than ever. *The New York Times* reported that one-third of newlyweds set up housekeeping on less than $60 a week, and one in ten couples ended up moving in with their families. One sociologist observed that couples were passing from the sheltered high school or college life into the stark realities of marriage with little or no life experience. He predicted a dramatic rise in the divorce rate.

For that and probably many other reasons, divorce did hit a peak of 5.3 per thousand marriages in 1979. But in the age of AIDS, a new traditionalism may be taking hold. The divorce rate has fallen and a 1991 Gallup poll showed marital fidelity may be on the rise.

New bride Traci Carr Fuller, 25, above, and her 30-year-old husband, Mark, definitely see marriage as a permanent commitment. "We waited a long time to get married, because we wanted to make sure that it was right," says Traci, who is seen tossing her bouquet at Atlanta's Rhodes Hall. "We would never get married unless we thought it would be forever."

"He can't last. I tell you flatly, he can't last."

*— Comedian Jackie Gleason, commenting on the
Elvis Presley phenomenon in the 1950s*

In 1954, Elvis Aaron Presley was a 19-year-old truck driver earning $35 a week in Memphis, Tennessee. Two years later, under the management of "Colonel" Tom Parker, he was the king of rock 'n roll.

Presley's velvet voice, sneering, sexy attitude and shocking hip gyrations sold 13.5 million singles and nearly three million albums in 1956 alone, but that was only part of the Elvis bonanza. That same year, fans shelled out $20 million for Elvis merchandise in outlets like the Kitty Kelly Shoe Store, above, right, in Louisville, Kentucky. "Official" Elvis merchandise ranged from jeans, jewelry, statuettes and dolls to bubblegum cards, rings, perfume and lipstick in shades of Tutti Frutti Red and Hound Dog Orange.

More than a decade after Presley's death, Elvis merchandise is selling better than ever, and his former Memphis home, Graceland, has become a secular shrine for millions of die-hard fans. Graceland-bound fans looking for relics of The King can browse in stores like this Memphis newsstand for Presley mugs, license plates, statuette-decanters with screw-on Elvis heads, commemorative plates and "Love Me Tender" milk bath and shampoo.

Elvis Presley memorabilia, Kitty Kelly Shoe Store, Louisville, Kentucky, by Stern Bramson, November 9, 1956

Elvis Presley memorabilia, Memphis, Tennessee, by Torin Boyd

The Brennan family, Oak Park, Illinois, March 26, 1959

In March, 1959, the 13-member Brennan family posed smartly in front of their home in Oak Park, Illinois. The Brennans were all decked out for Chicago's annual Michigan Avenue Easter Parade in clothes designed and sewn by their father, Thomas Brennan, the owner of a heating equipment business. For 17 years, Mr. Brennan tailored his family's Easter suits as a hobby. Starting just after Christmas, he would select a different theme each year. One year it was "the Dublin look," another year, "the Kennedy look."

The Brennan family, Oak Park, Illinois, by Dana Fineman

Mr. and Mrs. Brennan have since passed away, but eight of the
eleven Brennan children, their wives, husbands and ten children
gathered for the portrait above on September 29, 1991.
Coincidentally, photographer Dana Fineman made this portrait on the
day before the last Brennans left the old family home.

Above, The Cock 'n Bull, New York, New York, The Daily Mirror, November 14, 1959
Right, CBGB, New York, New York, by Douglas Kirkland

Rebels against the prim, middle-class morality and materialism of the post-war years, the Beats, above, flocked to the cafes and coffeehouses of San Francisco's North Beach and New York's Greenwich Village. Clad in leather jackets and tight jeans, they hung out in smoky clubs like The Cock 'n Bull, Caffe Cino and the Gaslight, listening to folk and jazz, sipping cappuccinos in mugs and nodding to the Beat verse of poets like Allen Ginsberg and Lawrence Ferlinghetti.

Over thirty years later, at CBGB, a rock club in Manhattan's Bowery area, musicians like Brian Childers, Alice Cohen and Paul Bearer, right, declare their own rebellion with dreadlocks, pierced noses and tattoos. Bands appearing at CBGB include avant-garde rockers like "Crawl Pappy," "Die Monster Die" and "Sheer Terror." Times change, the names change, but the idea is still the same—create a counterculture, shock society, shake up the world a bit.

I n the 1920s, swimming pools were splashy playthings for the rich. But by the 1950s, inexpensive construction techniques had brought pool prices within the range of middle-class homeowners. Industry promoters called backyard pools "a logical extension of the family television room," and cultural observers considered them a hallmark of the newly affluent America. The number of residential pools swelled from 30,000 in 1948 to 300,000 in 1963 and to over a million in the early '70s.

Right, Family at poolside, by H. Armstrong Roberts II, early 1960s

Today, 3.4 million American families have swimming pools in their backyards, ranging from shallow lap pools to extravagant, "natural" models featuring waterfalls and artificial rock. Peter and Donna Lance and their children, Christopher, four, and Mallory, two, splash in their 1950s, scallop-shaped pool in Los Angeles, which they've updated with a robotic pool sweep and a solar-powered cover.

Although backyard pools now seem to be an almost indispensible part of the Southern California good life, they pose problems as well. As the population burgeons, millions of pools put a strain on the water supply. And despite new safety precautions such as self-latching gates and alarm buoys that sense water movement, pool drownings are still the number one cause of accidental death among preschool children in California, Arizona and Florida.

Right, Family at poolside, Los Angeles, California, by Paul Chesley

Left, Tupperware party, photographer and location unknown, 1960
Above, Tupperware party, Roseville, California, by Alice G. Patterson

Every 2.7 seconds, from Munich to Miami Beach, there is a Tupperware party somewhere in the world. First marketed in 1945 by inventor Earl Tupper, the polyethylene Tupperware containers helped launch the plastics craze of the early 1950s. Wonderlier bowl sets, Spaghetti Dispensers, Pick-a-Deli lunch-meat containers and some 200 other products have made their way into 90 percent of American kitchens as well as 40 countries around the world. Fifteen of the earliest Tupperware designs are housed in the permanent design collection of New York's Museum of Modern Art.

Throughout the 1950s, '60s and '70s, the products were sold mostly by homemakers who made extra income hosting two-hour daytime Tupperware Home Parties for their friends. As in the 1960 get-together, left, this sales approach combined party games and contests with product demonstrations.

Tupperware is the fad that never died. Today, independent Tupperware manager Stephanie Garber, above, hosts shorter parties in the evening to accommodate the schedules of two-income families. Door prizes and "get-to-know-you" games like recipe swapping are still part of the Tupperware approach, but microwave cooking classes, food-freezing classes, "Rush Hour Parties" and environmental courses now account for a growing portion of sales. New products include microwave cooking containers, the Tortilla Keeper, marketed in Mexico, and the Kimono Keeper, sold only in Japan.

Pajama party, by Henry Grossman, 1963

In 1963, teenage girls had pajama parties, rolled their hair in jumbo, baby-pink curlers and listened to stacks of 45s on portable hi-fis. Paul and Paula, the Platters and Dion recorded heart-throb hits that year; Neil Sedaka and Bobby Rydell were popular and Chubby Checker had the nation twisting the night away. Most of the music of the time was pretty light and apolitical, but the times, they were a-changin'. Bob Dylan and Peter, Paul and Mary were already at the vanguard of American folk, and a recently formed English group, the Beatles, had just recorded the hit song "Love Me Do."

Girls with compact discs, Novato, California, by Jay O'Neil

oday, teenagers Vera Deatherage, Onya Vebrofski, Amy Buckner
and Wendy Morgan in Novato, California, are more likely to pop in a
cassette tape or compact disc than play an old-fashioned vinyl record.
They wear headphones, not curlers, and the music of the moment—
rap and hip-hop—is filled with political, social and cultural messages
as well as the usual love themes. Favorite bands on the day this picture
was taken included BBD, Boyz 2 Men, Yo-Yo, Hi Five and Public
Enemy. The girls, above, also mentioned that they would not be
caught dead in the "feet pajamas" like the ones in the "Then" picture.

Beatles fans, The Washington Post, *1964*

On "B-Day," February 7, 1964, Beatlemania swept America. Screaming, fainting, crying, frenzied fans mobbed New York's Kennedy Airport to catch a glimpse of four shaggy-headed lads who had already become a teenage obsession in Britain. John Lennon, 23, Paul McCartney, 21, George Harrison, 21, and Ringo Starr, 23, had already sold six million records. They scored the highest TV rating in U.S. history when they appeared on the "Ed Sullivan Show" later that week. The Beatles ended their 33-day U.S. tour with a gross of $2.1 million. "America was fantastic," said Ringo. "They all seem out of their minds."

New Kids on the Block fans, by Richard Pasley for Lynn Goldsmith

Today—or at least at the time this book went to press—thousands of teenagers hysterically mob concerts of New Kids on the Block, a band that has sold more than 14 million albums since 1988. Hailing from Boston, the band's wholesome-looking Danny Wood, 21, Jonathan Knight, 22, Jordan Knight, 20, Joe McIntyre, 18, and Donnie Wahlberg, 21, blend Motown and Main Street in a formula that has made them one of the most financially successful groups in the history of pop music. The band takes in $125,000 a night at sold-out concerts across the country and earns millions more in lucrative licensing agreements for products ranging from lunch boxes to breakfast cereal. Los Angeles radio programmer Steve Rivers, for one, would not compare the New Kids to the Beatles musically. "But for those of us who remember the early stages of Beatlemania," he says, "the enthusiasm is very similar."

"The first time I saw St. Louis, I could have bought it for six million dollars, and it was the mistake of my life that I did not do it."

— Mark Twain, Life on the Mississippi

Founded by the French in 1764, St. Louis was the hub of America's westward expansion into the Louisiana Purchase and beyond in the early 19th century. To commemorate the westward migration, the Gateway Arch National Monument was erected on the Mississippi riverfront in 1965. The stainless-steel-clad, 630-foot arch was designed by the renowned Finnish architect Eero Saarinen, who won the commission in a design contest. It was photographed, above right, in 1967 from the window of the last Trans World Airlines Constellation on one of that airline's last propeller-driven passenger flights.

More than 2.5 million tourists a year visit the Gateway Arch today and ride the elevators inside its legs to the observation platform above the Mississippi. From the top of the arch, in the middle of America, the words of the French politician and writer Alexis de Tocqueville seem especially far-sighted, "Millions of men are marching at once toward the same horizon; their language, their religion, their manners differ; their object is the same. Fortune has been promised to them somewhere in the West, and to the West they go to find it…"

Gateway Arch, St. Louis, Missouri, March 22, 1967

Gateway Arch, St. Louis, Missouri, by Dana Fineman

1963

"*I have a dream that my four little children will one day live in a nation where they will not be judged by the color of their skin, but by the content of their character.*"

—*Dr. Martin Luther King, Jr.*

"March for Jobs and Freedom," Washington, D.C., August 28, 1963, by
Consolidated News Pictures

"We aim at the infinite and when our arrow falls to earth it is in flames."

— *Oliver Wendell Holmes, Jr.*

The body of President John F. Kennedy lies in state inside the Capitol rotunda, Washington, D.C., November 24, 1963, by Associated Press Wire Photo

"This country, with its institutions, belongs to the people who inhabit it. Whenever they shall grow weary of the existing government, they can exercise their constitutional right of amending it, or their revolutionary right to dismember or overthrow it."

— Abraham Lincoln, First Inaugural Address

March on the Pentagon, Washington, D.C., October 1967, by Bernie Boston

"Here men from the planet Earth first set foot upon the moon, July 1969, A.D. We came in peace for all mankind."

— Plaque left by the first men to walk on the moon

Edwin "Buzz" Aldrin, Sea of Tranquility, the Moon, by Neil Armstrong, July 20, 1969

WASHINGTON
Colville
56
Eastern Washington
54
Orting
80
Port Blakely
70
Skagit County
6
Seattle
71
168
169
194
Western Washington
78

OREGON
Baker County
227

COLORADO
Arvada
101
Denver
21
22
69
149
Leadville
28
29
Pueblo
68

CALIFORNIA
Hollywood
87
103
120
121
175
Los Angeles
118
119
149
206
Merced
95
Novato
211
Porterville
174
Rohnert Park
183
Roseville
209
San Diego County
73
San Francisco
45
94
127
147
South San Francisco
105
Yosemite Valley
82
83

NEVADA
Las Vegas
156
157

ARIZONA
Phoenix
141

TEXAS
Austin
142
143
Dallas
189
Fort Bliss
19
Marfa
126

WYOMING
Cheyenne
4
85
108
109
Newcastle
84

NEBRASKA
Cherry County
61
Comstock
31
East Custer County
31
Omaha
11
Oshkosh
61

SOUTH DAK
Lantry
100
Pine Ridge
46
47
Near Rapid
134
135

MINNESOTA
Minneapolis
63

ILLINOIS
Chicago
66
116
136
165
Oak Park
200
201

MISSOURI
St. Louis
90
215

IOWA
Grundy Center
152

INDIANA
Speedway
96
97

MICHIGAN
Grosse Pointe Shores
145
Highland Park
98
Southfield
153
Warren
191
Wayne
99

PENNSYLVANIA
Ellsworth
166
Enon Valley
93
Kennett Square
89
Philadelphia
58
59
91
137
Pittsburgh
74
76
167
Pottstown
52
53
Redington
106
Scranton
107
South Pittston
92
Unknown
88

MASSACHUSETTS
Boston
12
44
62

MAINE
Camden
163
Pumpkin Island
40
41

CONNECTICUT
New Haven
42
43
New Preston
187
Unknown
162

NEW YORK
Catskills
228
Cooperstown
13
Coney Island
158
160
Garden City
186
Levittown
184
185
New York City
8
35
72
128
129
132
133
138
139
170
176
177
178
179
202
203

NEW JERSEY
Palisades Park
172
Woodcliff Lake
173

WASHINGTON, D.C.
15
17
25
27
110
111
115
130
131
192
216
218
220

MARYLAND
Annapolis
50
51
Baltimore
65
Andrews AFB
171

NORTH CAROLINA
Raleigh
141

KENTUCKY
Louisville
196
199

SOUTH CAROLINA
Summerville
2

TENNESSEE
Chattanooga
48
49
Dyersburg
113
Memphis
104
199
Mengelwood
112

FLORIDA
Cape Canaveral
181
Daytona Beach
150
151
Everglades
32
Miami
33
117
123
124
154
155

GEORGIA
Atlanta
197

Selected Bibliography

Academic American Encyclopedia. PRODIGY® interactive personal service. Danbury, CT: Grolier Electronic Publishing, Inc., 1990, 1991, 1992.

Aikman, Lonelle. *We, the people: The Story of the United States Capitol, Its Past and Its Promise*. Washington, D.C.: United States Capitol Historical Society, in cooperation with the National Geographic Society, 1978.

Allsop, Kenneth. *Bootleggers and Their Era*. New York: Doubleday, 1961.

Andrist, Ralph K. and the Editors of American Heritage. *American Heritage History of the Confident Years 1865-1916*. New York: American Heritage/Bonanza Books, 1987.

Andrist, Ralph K. and the Editors of American Heritage. *American Heritage History of the 20's & 30's*. New York: American Heritage Publishing Company, 1970.

Bader, Robert Smith. *Prohibition in Kansas*. Lawrence, KS: University of Kansas Press, 1986.

Bailey, Thomas and David M. Kennedy. *American Pageant: A History of Republics*. Lexington, MA: D. C. Heath & Company, 1983.

Barker, Bill and Jackie Lewis. *Denver!* New York: Doubleday & Company, 1972.

Beebe, Lucius and Charles Clegg. *San Francisco's Golden Era: A Picture of San Francisco Before the Fire*. Berkeley, CA: Howell-North, 1960.

Bimba, Anthony. *The Molly Maguires*. New York: International Publishers, 1932.

Black, Sheila. *Sitting Bull and the Battle of the Little Bighorn*. Englewood Cliffs, NJ: Silver Burdett Press, 1989.

Bohn, Dave and R. Petsheck. *Kinsey—Photographer: Locomotive Portraits*. San Francisco, CA: Chronicle Books, 1984.

Boorstin, Daniel J. *The Americans—The National Experience*. New York: Random House, 1965.

Boyer, Richard and David Savageua. *Your Guide to Finding the Best Places to Live in America*. Chicago, IL: Rand McNally, 1981.

Brooks, John. *Telephone: The First Hundred Years*. 1st Edition. New York: Harper & Row, 1976.

Brown, Dee. *Bury My Heart at Wounded Knee. An Indian History of the American West*. New York: Bantam, 1972.

Brown, Ezra and Wilfred Owen, and the Editors of Time-Life Books. *Wheels*. New York: Time-Life Books, 1967.

Bryan, C. D. B. and Glenn Albin. *In the Eye of Desert Storm: Photographers of the Gulf War*. New York: Harry N. Abrams, Inc., in association with the Professional Photography Division of Eastman Kodak Company, 1991.

Burchard, Sue. *The Statue of Liberty—Birth to Rebirth*. New York: Harcourt, Brace, Jovanovich, 1985.

Burns, M.D., Stanley B. *Masterpieces of Medical Photography from the Burns Archive*. Pasadena, CA: Twelve Trees Press, 1987.

Cable, Mary and the Editors of American Heritage. *American Manners & Morals: A Picture History of How We Behaved and Misbehaved*. New York: American Heritage Publishing Company, Inc., 1969.

Carlson, Richard and Bruce Goldman. *2020 Visions: Long View of a Changing World*. Stanford, CA: Stanford Alumni Association, 1990.

Carruth, Gorton and Eugene Ehrlich. *The Harper Book of American Quotations*. New York: Harper & Row, 1988.

Cassady, Steven. *Spanning the Gate*. Mill Valley, CA: Baron Wholman Squarebooks, 1979.

Cather, Willa. *My Antonia*. Boston: Houghton Mifflin Company, 1954.

Cather, Willa. *O Pioneers!* Boston: Houghton Mifflin Company, 1917.

Chancellor, Paul and Marjorie Wendall Potts. *A History of Pottstown Pennsylvania*. Pottstown, PA: Historical Society of Pottstown, 1953.

Clark, Arthur C. and the Editors of Time-Life Books. *Man And Space*. New York: Time-Life Books, 1969.

Coit, Margaret L. and the Editors of Life. *The Life History of the United States: The Sweep Westward*. Vol. 4. 1829-1849. New York: Time Inc., 1963.

Conrat, Maisie and Richard Conrat. *The American Farm: A Photographic History*. San Francisco: California Historical Society, San Francisco/Houghton Mifflin Company, 1977.

The Constitution of the United States of America. Philadelphia, PA, 1787.

Corn, Joseph J. and Brian Horrigan. *Yesterday's Tomorrows: Past Visions of the American Future*. New York: Summit Books, 1984.

Cudmore, Ginny and Jim Nelson, eds. *Timberlake & Area: 1910-1985*. Pierre, SD: State Publishing Company, with grant assistance from the South Dakota Committee on the Humanities, 1984.

Daniel, Clifton and John W. Kirshon, et al., eds. *Chronicle of America*. Mount Kisko, NY: Chronicle Publications, Inc., 1987.

Daniel, Pete and Raymond Smock. *A Talent for Detail: Photos of Miss Francis Benjamin Johnson*. New York: Harmony Books, 1974.

Davidson, Marshall B. and the Editors of American Heritage. *The American Heritage History of the Writers' America*. New York: American Heritage Publishing Company, Inc., 1973.

Davis, Mila. *City of Quartz: Excavating the Future in Los Angeles*. London: Vergo Press, 1990.

De Cock, Lilliane and Ronald McGee. *James Vander Zee*. New York: Morgan & Morgan, 1973.

Delaney, Edmund T. *New York's Greenwich Village*. Barre, MA: Barre Publishers, 1968.

de Tocqueville, Alexis. *Democracy in America*. Edited by Richard D. Heffner. New York: Penguin Group, 1956.

Doty, Robert, ed. *Photography in America*. New York: Random House, 1974.

Durham, Michael. *The Smithsonian Guide to Historic America—The Mid-Altantic States*. New York: Stewart, Tabori & Chang, 1989.

Editors of Time-Life Books. *This Fabulous Century—Prelude: 1870-1900 and Vols. I-VII, 1900-1970*. New York: Time-Life Books, 1969-1970.

Evers, Alf. *The Catskills: From Wilderness to Woodstock*. Garden City, NY: Doubleday Company, 1972.

Feininger, Andreas. *New York in the Forties*. New York: Dover Publications, Inc., 1978.

Finkel, Kenneth. *Philadelphia, Then And Now: 60 Sites Photographed in the Past and Present*. New York: Dover Publications, Inc., 1988.

Fite, Gilbert. *Mount Rushmore*. Norman, OK: University of Oklahoma Press, 1952.

Fitzgerald, F. Scott. *The Last Tycoon*. New York: Colliers Books/Macmillan Publishing Company, 1986.

Frost, H. Gordon. *I'm Frank Hamer—Life of a Texas Peace Officer*. Austin, TX: Pemberton Press, 1968.

Fulton, Marianne. *Eyes of Time: Photojournalism in America*. New York: George Eastman House, 1988.

Furnas, J.C. *The Americans: A Social History of the United States 1587-1914*. New York: G. P. Putnam's Sons, 1969.

Gans, Herbert J. *The Levittowners*. New York: Pantheon, 1967.

Garavagile, Louis A. and Charles G. Garavagile. *Guns in the American West*. Albuquerque, NM: University of New Mexico, 1984.

Gerber, Ellen W., Jan Felshin, Pearl Berlin, and Waneen Wyrick. *The American Woman in Sport*. Philippines: Addison-Wesley Publishing Company, 1974.

Golndinger, Carolyn, ed. *The Supreme Court at Work*. Washington, D.C.: Congressional Quarterly, 1990.

Gutman, Judith Mara. *Lewis W. Hine and the American Social Conscience*. New York: Walker Publishers, 1967.

Haggerty, James J., H. Guyford Stever, and the Editors of Time-Life Books. *Flight*. New York: Time-Life Books, 1971.

Hales, Peter B. *William Henry Jackson and the Transformation of the American Landscape*. Philadelphia, PA: Temple University Press, 1965.

Handlin, Oscar. *A Pictorial History of Immigration*. New York: Crown Publishers, Inc., 1972.

Harris, Jonathan. *A Statue for America: The First 100 Years of the Statue of Liberty*. New York: Four Winds Press, 1985.

Hartz, John, text. *New York in the 40's*. New York: Dover Publications, Inc., 1978.

Harvey, H. Thomas. *The Sequoias of Yosemite National Park*. San Jose, CA: Yosemite Association, 1978.

Hennessey, Julliette. *The United States Army Air Arm—April 1861 to April 1917*. Washington: Office of Air Force History, 1985.

Hogarth, James. *New York City*. Geneva, Switzerland: Nagel Publishers, 1973.

Holland, Jr., Francis Ross. *America's Lighthouses—Their Illustrated History Since 1716* Vermont: Steven Green Press, 1972.

Hoover, Gary, Alta Campbell, and Patrick J. Spain, eds. *Hoover's Handbook: Profiles of Over 500 Major Corporations*. Emeryville, CA: Publishers Group West, 1990.

Hudson, Patricia L. and Sandra L. Ballard, text. *The Smithsonian Guide to Historic America—The Carolinas and The Appalachian States*. New York: Stewart, Tabori & Chang, 1989.

Irwin, Inez Hays. *The Story of the Women's Party*. New York: Harcourt & Brace, 1921.

Jacobs, David and Anthony E. Neville. *Bridges, Canals & Tunnels*. Washington D.C.: American Heritage Publishing Company in association with The Smithsonian Institution, 1968.

James, Jr., Theodore. *The Empire State Building*. New York: Harper & Row, 1975.

Jay, Ricky. *Learned Pigs and Fireproof Women*. New York: Random House, 1986.

Jensen, Oliver. *American Album: Rare Photographs Collected by the Editors of American Heritage*. New York: American Heritage, 1968.

Johnson, Paul C. *Pictorial History of California*. Garden City, NY: Doubleday & Company, 1960.

Johnson, Paul C. and Richard Reinhardt. *San Francisco: As It Is, As It Was*. United States: Doubleday & Company, 1979.

Jolivson, James Weldon. *Black Manhattan*. New York: Athenum, 1975.

Jordan, Robert Paul. *The Civil War*. Washington, D.C.: National Geographic Society, 1969.

Jordan, Teresa. *Cowgirls: Women of the American West*. Garden City, NY: Doubleday & Company, 1982.

Josephy, Jr., Alvin M., ed. *The American Heritage Book of Indians*. New York: American Heritage Publishing Company, 1961.

Junge, Mark. *J. E. Stimson: Photographer of the West*. Lincoln, NE: University of Nebraska, 1985.

Ketchem, Richard M., ed. *The American Heritage Book of the Pioneer Spirit*. New York: American Heritage Publishing Company, 1959.

Knepp, Don. *Las Vegas: The Entertainment Capital*. Menlo Park, CA: Lane Publishing, 1987.

Lehman, Nicholas. *The Promised Land: The Great Migration and How It Changed America*. New York: Knopf, 1991.

Lehnartz, Klaus. *New York in the Sixties*. New York: Dover Publications, 1978.

Leibs, Chester H. *Main St. to Miracle Mile—American Roadside Architecture*. Boston: Little, Brown & Company, 1985.

Lencek, Lena and Gideon Bosker. *Making Waves*. San Francisco: Chronicle Books, 1989.

Lesy, Michael. *Wisconsin Death Trip*. New York: Anchor Books/Doubleday, 1973.

Letts, Vanessa. *New York*. Victoria Ingle, ed. New York: Cadogan Books Ltd., 1991.

Leuchtenburg, William E. and the Editors of Life. *The Life History of the United States: New Deal and Global War. Vol. 11, 1877-1890*. New York: Time Inc., 1964.

Leuchtenburg, William E. *The Life History of the United States: The Great Age of Change. Vol. 12, From 1945*. New York: Time Inc., 1964.

Lingeman, Richard. *Don't You Know There's A War On? The American Home Front 1941-1945*. New York: Putnam, 1970.

Logan, William Bryant and Susan Ochshorn, text. *The Smithsonian Guide to Historic America—The Pacific States*. New York: Stewart, Tabori & Chang, 1989.

Logan, William Bryant and Vance Muse, text. *The Smithsonian Guide to Historic America—The Deep South.* New York: Stewart, Tabori & Chang,1989.

Lord, Mark. *Combat Uniforms of the Civil War.* New York: Mallard Press, 1990.

Luchetti, Cathy and Carol Olwell. *Women of the West.* St. George, UT: Antelope Island Press, 1982.

Lynd, Robert S. and Helen Merrill Lynd. *Middletown: A Study in American Culture.* New York: Harcourt, Brace & Company, 1924.

Makower, Joel, ed. *The American History Source Book.* New York : Prentice Hall Press, 1988.

May, Ernest R. and the Editors of Life. *Life History of the United States:The Progressive Era. Vol. 9, 1901-1917.* New York: Time Inc., 1964.

May, Ernest R. and the Editors of Life. *Life History of the United States: War Boom & Bust. Vol. 10, 1933-1945.* New York: Time Inc., 1964.

Mayer, Martin. *The Schools.* New York: Harper & Brothers, 1961.

McConnell, Jane and Burt McConnell. *The White House—A History With Pictures.* New York: The Studio Publications, Inc., in association with Thomas Y. Crowell Company, 1954.

Miller, Terry. *Greenwich and How It Got That Way.* New York: Crown Publishers, Inc., 1987.

Mingo, Jack and John Javna. *The Whole Pop Catalog/The Berkeley Pop Culture Project.* New York: Avon Books, 1991.

Moscow, Henry. *The Street Book: An Encyclopedia of Manhattan's Street Names and Their Origin.* Edited by Thomas Tracy: Hagstrom Company, Inc.,1978.

Mott, Frank Luther. *American Journalism: A History of Newspapers in the United States through 250 Years, 1690-1940.* New York: Macmillan Company, 1941.

Mott, Frank Luther. *The News in America.* Cambridge, MA: Harvard University Press, 1962.

Murphy, Francis, ed. *Walt Whitman: The Complete Poems.* England: Penguin Books, 1977.

NASA. Information Summaries/PMS 018-A (KSC). *Countdown! NASA Launch Vehicles Facilities.* John F. Kennedy Space Center, FL: NASA, 1989.

NASA. Facts/KSC #49-85. *Landing the Shuttle at KSC.* John F. Kennedy Space Center, FL: NASA, 1985.

NASA. Fact Sheet/KSC #68-88. *NASA's Orbiter Fleet: Columbia, Discovery, Atlantis.* John F. Kennedy Space Center, FL: NASA, 1988.

National Baseball Hall of Fame & Museum, Inc., National Baseball Library, and Gerald Astor. *The Baseball Hall of Fame 50th Anniversary Book.* New York: Prentice Hall, 1988.

The National Cyclopaedia of American Biography. Vol. XXI. Edited by distinguished biographers. New York: James T. White & Company, 1931.

Neft, David S. and Richard M. Cohen. *The World Series.* New York: St. Martin's Press, 1990.

Nellor, John H., introduction. *Oregon and National School Facts.* Portland, OR: Oregon Educational Association, 1961.

Novotny, Ann. *Alice's World: The Life and Photography of An American Original—Alice Austen, 1866-1952.* Old Greenwich, CT: Chatham Press, 1976.

O'Brien, Robert, Edward V. Lewis, and the Editors of Time-Life Books. *Ships.* New York: Time-Life Books, 1970.

O'Neil, Edward. *Rollerskating.* New York: Ronald Press Company, 1960.

Paden, Irene D. *The Wake of the Prairie Schooner.* New York: Macmillan Company, 1947.

Paler, Stanley W. *Las Vegas: As It Began—As It Grew.* Edited by Philip Cecchettini. Las Vegas, NV: Nevada Publishers, 1971.

Panati, Charles. *Panati's Parade of Fads, Follies, and Manias.* New York: HarperPerennial, a division of HarperCollins, 1991.

Peterson, Nancy M. *The People of The Moonshell—A Western River Journal.* Frederick, CO: Renaissance House, 1984.

Place, Stan Campbell. *The Art and Science of Professional Makeup.* New York: Milady Publishing Company, 1989.

Ploski, Harry A. and James Williams, eds. *The Negro Almanac: A Reference Work on the African-American.* 5th ed. Detroit: Gale Research, Inc.,1989.

Plumbe, Jr., John. *The Presidents' House (White House).* Washington, D.C.: Plumbe Daguerreotypes, lot 11338, ca.1846.

Pourade, Richard F. *The Glory Years: The History of San Diego.* San Diego, CA: The Union-Tribune Publishing Company, 1964.

Powelson, Mark K. and Pamela Feinsilber, eds. *The Golden Gate Bridge 50th Anniversary.* San Francisco: *San Francisco Focus,* a publication of KQED, Inc., 1987.

Probert, Christina. *Brides in Vogue since 1910.* New York: Abbeville Press, Inc., 1984.

Probert, Christina. *Swimwear in Vogue since 1910.* Abbeville Press, Inc., 1981.

Publications International Limited. *The Elvis Album.* Lincolnwood, IL: Publications International Limited, 1991.

Roberts, Ellwood, ed. *Biographical Annals of Montgomery County, PA.* New York: T.S. Benham and Company and the Lewis Publishing Company,1904.

Rothstein, Arthur. *The Depression Years As Photographed by Arthur Rothstein.* New York: Dover Publications, 1978.

Sandburg, Carl. *Harvest Poems 1910-1960.* Orlando, FL: Harcourt, Brace & World, 1960.

Sandler, Martin W. *American Image: Photographing One Hundred Years in the Life of a Nation.* Chicago, IL: Contemporary Books, Inc.,1989.

Schlesinger, Jr., Arthur M., ed. *The Almanac of American History.* New York: G. P. Putnam's Sons, 1983.

Schoener, Allon. *The Italian Americans.* Commentary by A. Bartlett Giamatti. New York: Macmillan Publishing Company, 1987.

Seldenbaum, Art. *Los Angeles 200: A Bicentennial Celebration.* New York: Harry N. Abrams, Inc., 1980.

Shaw, Renata V., ed. *A Century of Photographs 1846-1946.* Washington, D.C.: Library of Congress, 1980.

One-room schoolhouse, Baker County, Oregon, by Dorothea Lange, October, 1939

Shnayerson, Robert. *Illustrated History of the Supreme Court of the United States.* New York: Harry N. Abrams, Inc., 1986.

Shumway, George, Edward Durrell, and Howard C. Frey. *The Conestoga Wagon 1750-1850.* York, PA: Early American Industries Association, 1964.

Slide, Anthony. *The Big V: A History of the Vitagraph Company.* Metuchen, NJ: Scarecrow Press, Inc., 1987.

Smiley, Nixon. *Yesterday's Florida.* Miami, FL: E. A. Seemann Publishing, Inc., 1974.

Smith, Arthur G. *Pittsburgh: Then and Now.* Pittsburgh, PA: University of Pittsburgh Press, 1990.

Smith, Rex Alan. *Moon of Popping Trees.* New York: Readers Digest Press, 1975.

Snow, Edward Rowe. *The Lighthouses of New England 1716-1973.* New York: Dodd, Mead & Company, 1973.

Spiering, Frank. *Bearer of a Million Dreams: The Biography of the Statue of Liberty.* Ottowa, IL: Jameson Books, 1965.

Stratton, Joanna L. *Pioneer Women: Voices from the Kansas Frontier.* New York: Simon & Schuster, 1981.

Sukenick, Ronald. *Down and In: Life in the Underground.* New York: Beach Tree Books, 1987.

Taylor, John, ed. *North American Railroads.* New York: Crescent Books, 1991.

Tebeau, Charlton W. *A History of Florida.* Coral Gables, FL: University of Miami Press, 1971.

Toll, Jean Barth and Michael Schwager, eds. *Montgomery County—The Second Hundred Years.* Norristown, PA: Montgomery County Federation of Societies, 1983.

Torrence, Bruce. *Hollywood's 100 Years.* Hollywood, CA: Hollywood Chamber of Commerce & Steve Fiske Enterprises, 1979.

Trachtman, Paul and the Editors of Time-Life Books. *The Gunfighters.* Alexandria, VA: Time-Life, 1974.

USGPO. *The Capitol: A Pictorial History of the Capitol and of the Congress.* 7th Ed. Washington, D.C.: USGPO, 1979.

Van Haften, Julia. *From Talbot to Steiglitz: Masterpieces of Early Photography from the New York Public Library.* New York: Thames & Hudson, Inc., 1982.

Van Zant, Eleanor. *Enjoying Skating.* United States: Paddington Press, 1978.

Ward, Geoffrey C., with Ric Burns and Ken Burns. *The Civil War: An Illustrated History.* New York: Alfred A. Knopf, Inc., 1990.

Warren, James R. *Where Mountains Meet the Sea, An Illustrated History of Puget Sound.* United States: Windsor Publications, 1986.

Weisberger, Bernard A. and the Editors of Life. *The Life History of the United States: Age of Steel & Steam. Vol. 7, 1877-1890.* New York: Time Inc., 1964.

Weisberger, Bernard A. and the Editors of Life. *The Life History of the United States: Reaching For Empire. Vol. 8, 1890-1901.* New York: Time Inc., 1964.

Wenborn, Neil. *The U.S.A: A Chronicle in Pictures.* New York: Smithmark Publishers Inc., 1991.

Wilder, Thornton. *Our Town.* New York: Harper & Row, 1957.

Wright, Barton. *The Hopi Photographs: Kate Cory. 1905-1912.* La Canada, CA: Chaco Press, 1986.

Acknowledgements

Catskill Mountains, New York, late 19th century

Picture Sources

Bernie Boston, pp. 220-221

The Bettmann Archive, UPI and New York Daily Mirror Collections, pp. 115 Top, 116, 144, 162 Left, 176, 184, 190, 200, 202

Bison Archives, pp. 103 Top, 120

The Boeing Company, pp. 168, 169

Boston Public Library, pp. 11, 62

Brown Brothers, pp. 86, 128

The Burns Archive, courtesy Stanley B. Burns, M.D., p. 65

Caterpillar Tractor Company, pp. 54-55

Colorado State Historical Society, p. 149 Top

Culver Pictures, pp. 158-159

Custom Medical Stock Photography, pp. 66-67

Denver Public Library, Western History Collection, pp. 21, 28

The District of Columbia Public Library, Washington Post Collection, p. 212

The Estate of James Van Der Zee, p. 132

Florida State Archives, pp. 123, 150, 154

Ford Motor Company, p. 98

Frinzi Studios, p. 43 Right

General Electric Company/U.S. Army Ordnance, p. 181 Top

General Motors, p. 191 Right

Golden Gate Bridge, Highway and Transportation District, p. 147 Top

H. Armstrong Roberts, pp. 178, 205

Hagley Museum and Library, pp. 106, 135 Top, 166

Indianapolis Motor Speedway Corporation, pp. 96, 97 Right

The International Museum of Photography at George Eastman House, pp. 8-9, 18, 72, 88, 92

LGI Photo Agency, p. 213

Library of Congress, Prints and Photographs Division, Cover and pp. 1, 2-3, 12, 32, 40, 44, 46, 48, 52, 68, 82, 90, 94, 104, 110, 138, 152, 156, 182, 186, 227, 228

The Library Company of Philadelphia, p. 58

Life Picture Service (all from Life Magazine © Time Warner, Inc.), pp. 172, 174, 188, 193, 210

Los Angeles County Museum of Natural History, Seaver Center for Western History, p. 118

Magnum, p. 73 Right

NASA, Johnson Space Center, pp. 222-223

The National Archives, pp. 130, 136, 165 Top, 170

National Geographic Society, courtesy of U.S. Supreme Court Historical Society, p. 27

Nebraska State Archives, Solomon D. Butcher Collection, pp. 31 Top, 61 Top

The New-York Historical Society, pp. 34-39 Top Gatefold

New York State Historical Association, Cooperstown, p. 13

The Office of The Architect of the U.S. Capitol, p. 15

Orange County Historical Society, Orlando, Florida, p. 230

Pennsylvania Historical and Museum Commission, pp. 74-75

Roger Scruggs Films, p. 181 Bottom

San Francisco Maritime Museum, Wilhelm Hester Collection, p. 70 Left

Sipa Press, p. 127

Staten Island Historical Society, Alice Austen Collection, p. 50

Supreme Court of the United States, pp. 24, 25

Sygma, p. 171

Timber Lake and Area Historical Society, p. 100

Trans World Airlines, Inc., p. 215 Top

Tupperware Home Parties, p. 208

Uniphoto, pp. 216-217

University of Louisville Photographic Archives, pp. 112, 196, 199 Top

University of North Carolina Library at Chapel Hill, North Carolina Collection, p. 141 Top

University of Texas at Austin, Barker Texas History Center, p. 142

University of Texas at Austin, Harry Ransom Humanities Research Center, p. 126

The Washington Blade, p. 131

Whatcom Museum of History and Art, D. Kinsey Collection, pp. 6-7, 79, 232

Wide World Photos, pp. 218-219

Wyoming State Archives, Museums and Historical Department, pp. 4-5, 85 Top, 108

Yale University Library, Manuscripts Division, p. 42

Organizations

Literally hundreds of organizations and individuals cooperated in the making of this book. They have our sincere gratitude.

Abrams & Associates
American Airlines
American Heritage Library
American Photo Archive
American Swedish Institute
America's Funniest Home Videos
Arch
ARCO, Photograph Department
Aspen Historical Society
Austin Public Library, Austin History Center
The Bank of America, Mill Valley, California
Beacon Historical Society
Beltrami County Historical Society
Big Bend Sentinel
The Boston Athenaeum
Boston Public Library
Broken Bow Historical Society
Brown Brothers
BWC Photolabs
Camera Hawaii
The Carbon Alternative
Carnegie Branch for Local History (Boulder)
Carnegie County Historical Society
Carpenter Center of Photography Archive
Castle Air Force Base
Center for Creative Photography
Champion Paper Corporation
Chattanooga Regional History Museum
Chesapeake Bay Maritime Museum
Chevy Chase Historical Society
The Chicago Historical Society
The Chrysler Building
Colorado Springs Gazette
Colt Manufacturing Company
Culver Pictures
Consolidated Coal
Curt Teich Postcard Archives/
    Lake County Museum
Dallas Historical Society
Douglas County Museum of History
Ford Motor Company
The Free Library of Philadelphia
Fresno City & County Historical Society
Gale Memorial Library
Gallatin County Historical Society
Galveston Park Board of Trustees
Goldbeck Company
Gold's Gym, Hollywood, California
Grand County Historical Association
Gymboree
Harris County Heritage Society
Hawaiian Historical Society
Henry Ford Museum & Greenfield Village
Hidalgo County Historical Museum
Historical Society of Washington, D.C.
ICS
Immigrant City Archives
Indian Hill Historical Society
Ippolito's
Ivey Seright International
Johns Hopkins University

Kennedy Space Center
KGBC, Galveston
King King Restaurant, Hollywood, California
Koochiching County Historical Society
KTSP-TV, Channel 10, Phoenix, AZ
The Library Company, Philadelphia
Lindenbaum & Associates
Los Angeles Public Library, History Department
Louisiana State University, Shreveport Archives
Maine State Archives
Matteson Historical Society
The Miami-Dade Public Library
Museum of New Mexico
NASA, Kennedy Space Center
National Anthropological Archives,
    Smithsonian Institution
The National Archives, Still Pictures Branch
National Geographic Society
National Museum of Roller Skating
The National Organization for Women
The National Park Service, Mt. Rushmore
Nez Perce County Historical Society
NW Transport Service, Inc.
New York City Department of Transportation,
    Bureau of Bridges
New York City Film Permit Office
Orange County Historical Museum, Florida
Pacific Bell
Park Forest Historical Society
Pasadena Public Library
Peale Museum, Baltimore City Life Museum
The Pennsylvania Historical Society
Piggly Wiggly
Pinnacle Publishing Services
The Pottstown Police Department
Putnam County Archives and History Commission
Railway & Locomotive Historical Society, Inc.
Rhode Island Museum of Art
H. Armstrong Roberts
Roger Scruggs Films
The Rose Art Museum, Brandeis University
St. John's Hospice
Samy Salon System
San Francisco Maritime Museum
The San Francisco Public Library
The Seaver Institute of Western History
Shrimp Boat Restaurant
The Signal Hill Public Library
Silviane Pagent Productions
Smith Library of Regional History
Soup To Nuts Catering, El Cerrito, California
Southbury Historical Society, Inc.
Sullivan County Chamber of Commerce
Taliaferro County Historical Society
Tom Bradley International Airport
Tupperware Home Parties
Tuskegee University
The Union Pacific Railroad
United States Army Ordnance
United States Army, 3rd Cavalry Regiment
The United States Capitol Police
United States Drug Enforcement Agency
US Geologic Library
United States Naval Academy
United States Postal Office,
    Hollywood, California

Virginia Commonwealth University
Washington State Historical Society
Wells Fargo Bank, Mill Valley Branch
Western Hardware Company,
    Museum & Emporium
West Virginia University Library,
    West Virginia and Regional History Collection
White Pillars Museum
The Women's Civic League of Cheyenne,
    Wyoming
Workman & Temple Family Homestead Museum
Yale Sports Information

Consultants, Friends and Advisors

Joseph Abrams
Heather Akawie
Leslie S. Alberti
Irenio Alejo
Buddy Allen
Peter Allen
Billy Amberg
Mike Ames
Enriquez Analia
James C. Anderson
Lois Anderton
Norma Jean Andrew
Tom & Mary Angelo
Himawana Apiwibowo
The Balkan Apollos
Diana Arecco
Ken Ariolo, Capt., USAF
Susan Arkin
Edward Armstrong
Mea Arnold
Bob Arnott
Larry M. Asbell
Herb and Dorothy Ascherman
Paul Ash
Rebecca Atkinson
Dr. W.F. Atwater
Maria Victoria Auge
Steven Autchison
Chris Baer
Joey Baldino
Regina Baldino
Anna Maria Bambara
Michael Banks
Robert Banks
Judith Banning
Adelaide Barbey
Bill Barlow
Caroline Barnes
Marilyn Barnes
Audrey Barnhart
Michelle Barr
Ralff Barr
Jenny Barry
W. Henry Bass
Nancy Bath
Judy Battaglia
Paul Bearer
Guillermo Beauchamp
Tina Bechler
Andy & Sam Belt
Eliane Benisti
Kevin Bentley
Mark Berger
Rod Bergiel
Michel A. Bergman
Steve Berl
Luigi Bernabo
Pam Beyers
Bipin, Bharti, Prashant & Samit Bhayani
Carole Bidnick

P.P. Kamdar
Vinu, Chitra, Paresh &
   Viren Kamdar
Loretta A. Kane
Marita Kankowski
D. Madeline Kaphengst
Bruce Karstad
Ami Kassar
Andrew Katz
Melissa Katz
Phyllis Katz
Debi Kee-Biggers
Leslie Keenan
Randy Keis
Jess H. Keller
Rachel, Tom, Lisa &
   Ben Kellerman
Patricia Kelly
Tom Kelly
Emory Kemp
David Kent
Walter Kidney
Soo Hwan Kim
Henry Kimmel
Charles King
Henry Kirby
Francoise Kirkland
Sylviane Sidney Kitchen
Judy, Sandy, Lauren & Alana
   Kivowitz
Benjamin Klahr
Sophia Klahr
Doug Kline
Pam Kline
Mark Klingelhoffer, Capt.
Tim Knapp
Ernst Knudsen
Jeff Koehler
Hiroko Koff
Karen Konecky
Andy Kopra
Ryan Kowalske
David and Marla Kremer
Jeffrey F. Kriendler
Gary Krumweide
Jonathan Kuhn
Linda Kulik
Raymond P. Kuper
Joseph H.Kushner, M.D.
Jane Labys
Karla Lacey
Laura Lacuira
Eliane Laffont
Robert Laffont
Beverly LaFrance
Keith LaLonde
Kathy Lamb
Linda Lamb
Amanda Marie LaMont
Eric LaMont
Lauren LaMont
Christopher Lance
Donna Lance
Mallory Lance
Mary Lance
Mr. and Mrs. Peter Lance
   and Family
Sonia Land
Robin Lande
Ralph Lantigua
Jose Latosa
Cindy Lazar
Joseph Leander-Schneider
Billie Jeanne Lebda
Judy LeBlanc
Carole Lee
Terry LeGoubin
Mario Leiva
Carla Leo
Pete Lesher
Jackie Leventoff
Richard Levick
Scott Levin
Aaron Levinson
Bonnie Levinson

Mr. & Mrs. James Levinson
Susan Levinthal
Brigid J. Lewis
Roger Licot
Jessica Lidgren
Sybil Lindenbaum
Becky Lintz
C.E. Llafet
Ann Lloyd
Tom & Susan Lloyd
Susan Lloyd & John Karrel
Charles London
Lois A. Long
Richard LoPinto
Barbara Loren
John Louden
Arlene B. Lowery
Jan D. Lowry
Leonard Lueras
Maricela Lujan
Anne H. Lukowski
Bernard Lumpkin
Mari and Walter Lurie
Chloe MacDonald
Andy MacInnes and Kathy Fong
Heather Mackintosh-Sims
Robert Macon
Janice Madhu
Susan Magnus
Steve Mah
Janice S. Mahaffey
Bill Maher
Karen Maldonado
Charles Mallone
Rick Mandelkorn
Courtney Mangus
Carol Mann
Charlotte Mansfield
Mary Markey
Brenda Marsh
Joan F. Marsh
Julie Marshall
Catherine A.Martin
Sara Renee Martin
Ana M. Martinez
Roxanna Martinez
William R. Massa, Jr.
Augie Mastrouguisepp
Akira Matsuura
Claudine Maugendre
Elvin L. Mauzey
David Maxey
Claire Maxwell
Melissa May
Brother Stanley MacNeil
Holloway McCandless
Mike McCarthy
Vernon H. McCaster
Ruth McCauley
Janice Hanzalik McCraken
Karen McCulloch
Mitzi A. McCune
Allie McDaniel
Bill McDaniel
Brian D. McDaniel
David McDaniel
Donald McDaniel
Hubert McDaniel
John H. McDaniel
Michelle McDaniel
Micki McDaniel
Minda Sue McDaniel
Nadine McDaniel
Sharon McDaniel
Tammy McDaniel
Tim McDaniel
Jane H. McGinley
Kim McGuire
Patricia Ann McMahon
Perry McMullin
Aubrey McNally
Sheri McNary
Robert McRae
Martha Mears
Esther Mehalow

Judith Meier
Greg Melconian
Clarice Melinkovich
Veronica Mellgren
Faviola Mendez
Doug, Teresa & Paolo Menuez
Roxanne Mick
Kathy Williams Mickelson
Robert John Mihovil
Don D. Mikelson
Kevin Mikowicz
Amy Miller
Cheryl Miller
Cynthia Reed Miller
Elaine Miller
Judy and Walter Miller
Lisa A. Miller
Lou Ann Miller
Dr. H.T. & Shirley Mills
Ronald V. Mills
Launa Newman Minson
Ida Mintz
Carlos A. Miranda
Linda J. Mitchel
Davita Mitchell
Jena Mitchell
Martha Miyamoto
Martin Miyamoto
Roger Miyamoto
Zandra Moberg
Kohei Mochizuki
John Moffitt
Phillip Moffitt
Shawn Moheb
Greg Monfils
Kevin Monko
Jason Monroe
Art Mont
Leigh Moore
Lindsay Moran
Alexandra Morehouse
Dolores Moreno
Adrian Morgan
Wendee Morgan
Arthur D. Morgenstern
Kim Morris
Ann Moscicki
Sarina Moss
Lydia E. Motsinger
Jennifer Mottola
Joseph Mottola
Michael Mottola
Rosemary Mottola
Barbara Moulton
Larry Mulkey
Jeremy Mullett
Jim Mulqueen
Dale Munsey
Debbie & John Murphy
Dindy Murphy
Tanya Narath
Jean Jacques Naudet
Peggy Nault
Dr. Michael Naumann
Ymelda Navajo
Maria D. Navia
Dr. Matthew Naythons
Joanna C. Nejad
Carrol C. Nelson
Dency L. Nelson
Dick Nelson
Jim Nelson
Grazia Neri
Kwok Biu Ng
Ray Ng
Catherine L. Nicholas
Peggy Nicholls
Jane Nicoll
Margo Nieves
Dianne Nilsen
Steve Nolan
Barbara Norfleet
Jody Norman
Eileen O'Connor
Larid Ogden

Bernard Ohenian
Beverly Olmstead
Valerie L. Olsen
Eric Ople
Beatrice Osapai
John O'Shea
John Owen
Susan Oyama
Illona Pagan
James S. Paine
Barbara Palazzolo
John Panter
Rick Pappas
J. P. Pappis
Scott Paré
Donny Parker
Jack & Gertrude Parker
Scarlette P. Parker, USAF
Lt. Col. David Partain
Micah Parzen
Richard Patch
Grady, Joah & Neffy Peck
Jim & Susan & Nellie Peck
Carmen, Roger, Ramona
   & Anita Pedersen
Cynthia Pelak
A. Perez
Aaron Perez
Gabe & Pat Perle
Liz Perle
James Perry
James, Margery, James, Jr.
   and Adriana Perry
Richard C. Perry
Reginia A. Perry, Ph.d.
Susan Jaret Pesko
Stacy K. Peter
Ann, Alec, Ross & Gus Peters
Sam Petersen
Beth Peterson
Paul D. Phillips
Suzanne Philpott
Pennie Pickering
Drummond Pike
Anthony Pisano
LawriePitcher Platt
Laurie Platt
Robert Pledge
Ethan Pollack
Paula Pollock
Jim Popovich
Glenn Porter
Joy Powell
Jim Powerie
Anne Price
Rebecca Probasco
Youvet Profit
Seymour Proud
Steve Proud
Jacqueline J. Pryor
Susan Pulido
Cathy Qealy
Luis Alfreda Quezada
Raul & Judith Quezada
Robert Rabkin, M.D.
Dee-Dee Ranal
Barbara Belcher Rayborn
Schnita Rayborn
Sylvie Rebbot
Mary Regan
Larry Rehn
Susan S. Reich
Paul Repetto
Patrick D. Reynolds
Robert L. Rice
Renee P. Richard
Patti Richards
Sharon K. Richmeier
Ed Rider
Susie, Cornel, Christopher
   & Catherine Riklin
Julie A. Roberson
Richard Robinson
Susana Rodriguez
Diana "Danny" Roeseler

Dorian Rogers
David Rose
Pat Rose
Adam Rosen
Anne Rosen
Barbara Rosen
Florence & Louis Rosen
Joel Rosen
Lara Rosen
Sol & Florence Rosen
Sue, Bruce, Michael
   & Jonathan Rosen
Joan Rosenberg
ReidRossman
Janice & Lenny Roth
Lawrence Stephen Rotvold
Galen & Barbara Rowell
Jess A. Roybal
Ron Rubalcaba
Brett Rubel
Richard Rudisall
Michael Runzler
Roland C. Russell
Marion D. Russo
Tiffany Rutledge
Kathy Ryan
Pat Ryan
Mark Rykoff
Caitlin Saafield
Amy C. Sabin
Ruth Sackheim
Nola Safro
Scott, Bao & Benjamin Sagan
Bob Saget
Frank & Wanda Salerno
Marianne Samenko
Curt Sanburn
Will & Marta Sanburn
Edward Sanford
Mike Sanford
Nereida Santa-Cruz
Michael Santo
Nicole Gray Saybrook
Suezanne Scales
Dick Schaap
Charles & Joanna Schiedt
Aaron Schindler
Aaron Schmidt
David Schonauer
Betsy Schrott
Jessica Schultzman
Leonard D. Schutt
Dr. & Mrs. Leonard Schwartz
Kent Scott
Trey Scott
Rex Scouten
William Scoville
Robin Seaman
Krystal D. Sears
Dennis Seibel
Gary Serby
Rob & Annette Shapiro
Cathy Shepard
Pat Sheppard
Steve, Dana, Caty
   & Alex Sherman
Sykvia J. Sherman
Keva Sieber
Damon Silverman
Becky Simmons
Erin Simmons
Ethan Simon
Michael Singer
Nancy P. Sinsel
Margaret & Bill Sircher
Meghan, Molly & Sean Sircher
Michael Sisson
Rev. Francis Skelly
Silvia Sleight
Catherine W. Smith
Patricia C. Smith
Ronald Lee Smith
Cindy Soell
Sabrina Sojourner
Eva Solovay

Self-portrait, Darius Kinsey, c.1905

Staff & Photographers

232